AF280590

FSC
www.fsc.org

MIX

Papier aus ver-
antwortungsvollen
Quellen

Paper from
responsible sources

FSC® C105338

Stefan Henneken

USE OF THE **SOLID** PRINCIPLES
WITH THE **IEC 61131-3**

5 Principles for Object-Oriented Software Design
in the PLC Programming

Impressum

Bibliographic Information of the German National Library:
The German National Library lists this publication in the German National Bibliography; detailed bibliographic data are available on the Internet at http://dnb.dnb.de.

© 2023 Stefan Henneken (https://StefanHenneken.net)

2nd edition with minor corrections in November 2023

Production and publishing: BoD – Books on Demand, Norderstedt

ISBN: 978-3-7578-9222-7

1 Table of contents

2   Foreword

The SOLID principles are an essential part of object-oriented software development and have proven to be valuable tools for developing clean, maintainable and extensible code. In industrial automation technology, especially in the programming of controllers with IEC 61131-3, it is of particular importance to develop robust and reliable systems.

This book presents the SOLID principles in detail and explains them using examples in IEC 61131-3. It also illustrates how the application of these principles improves the maintainability, extensibility and reliability of software systems.

In addition to the SOLID principles, the KISS, DRY, LoD and YAGNI principles are also presented. Although these do not belong to the group of SOLID principles, they are a helpful addition to them.

I hope that this book will be useful to all those involved in industrial automation and that it can help you to develop better and more reliable systems. Thank you for choosing our book and good luck in applying SOLID principles in your work!

Stefan Henneken

3 SOLID – Five principles for better software

In addition to the syntax of a programming language and the understanding of the most important libraries and frameworks, other methodologies – such as design patterns – belong to the fundamentals of software development. Aside from a design pattern, design principles are also a helpful tool in the development of software. SOLID is an acronym for five such design principles, which help developers to design software more understandable, more fexible and more maintainable.

In larger software projects, a great number of function blocks exist that are connected to each other via inheritance and references. These units interact by the calls of the function blocks and their methods. The interaction of the code units can unnecessarily complicate the extending or finding of errors if designed wrongly. In order to develop sustainable software, the function blocks should be modeled in such a way that they are easy to extend.

Many design patterns apply the SOLID principles to suggest an architectural approach for the respective task. The SOLID principles are not to be understood as rules, but rather as advice. They are a subset of many principles that an American software engineer and lecturer Robert C. Martin (also known as Uncle Bob) presented in his book *Clean Architecture: A Craftsman's Guide to Software Structure and Design*. The SOLID principles include:

- **S**ingle Responsibility Principle (SRP)
- **O**pen/Closed Principle (OCP)
- **L**iskov Substitution Principle (LSP)
- **I**nterface Segregation Principle (ISP)
- **D**ependency Inversion Principle (DIP)

The principles shown here are hints that make it easier for a developer to improve code quality. The effort pays for itself after a short time, because changes will be easier, tests and debugging will be faster. Thus, the knowledge of these five design principles should be part of every software developer's basic knowledge.

3.1 Single Responsibility Principle (SRP)

A function block should have only one responsibility. If the functionality of a program is changed, this should have effects only on few function blocks. Many small function blocks are better than a few large ones. The code appears at first sight more extensive, but it is easier to organize. A program with many smaller function blocks, each for a special task, is easier to maintain, than few large function blocks, claiming to cover everything.

3.2 Open/Closed Principle (OCP)

According to the *Open/Closed Principle*, function blocks should be open for extensions but closed for changes. The implementation of extensions should only be achieved by adding code, not by changing existing code. A good example of this principle is inheritance. A new function block inherits from an existing function block. New functions can thus be added without having to change the existing function block. It is not even necessary to have the program code.

3.3 Liskov Substitution Principle (LSP)

Liskov Substitution Principle requires that derived function blocks must always be usable in place of their basic function blocks. Derived function blocks must behave like their basic function blocks. A derived function block may extend the base function block, but not restrict it.

3.4 Interface Segregation Principle (ISP)

Many customized interfaces are better than one universal interface. Accordingly, an interface may only contain those functions that really belong together closely. Comprehensive interfaces create links between otherwise independent program parts. Thus, the *Interface Segregation Principle* has a similar goal as the *Single Responsibility Principle*. However, there are different approaches to the implementation of these two principles.

3.5 Dependency Inversion Principle (DIP)

Function blocks are often linearly interdependent in one direction. A function block for logging messages calls methods of another function block to write data to a database. There is a fixed dependency between the function block for logging and the function block for accessing the database. The *Dependency Inversion Principle* resolves this fixed dependency by defining a common interface. This is implemented by the block for the database access.

In the following chapters, I will introduce the individual SOLID principles in more detail and try to explain them using an example. With each SOLID principle, I will try to optimize the program further.

4 The Dependency Inversion Principle

Fixed dependencies are one of the main causes of poorly maintainable software. Certainly, not all function blocks can exist completely independently of other function blocks. After all, these interact with each other and are thus interrelated. However, by applying the *Dependency Inversion Principle*, these dependencies can be minimized. Changes can therefore be implemented more quickly.

With a simple example, I will show how negative couplings can arise between function blocks. Then, I will resolve these dependencies with the help of the *Dependency Inversion Principle*.

4.1 Starting situation

The example contains three function blocks, each of which controls different lamps. While `FB_LampOnOff` can only switch a lamp on and off, `FB_LampSetDirect` can set the output value directly to a value from 0 % to 100 %. The third function block (`FB_LampUpDown`) is only able to relatively dim the lamp by 1 % using the `OneStepDown()` and `OneStepUp()` methods. The method `OnOff()` sets the output value immediately to 100 % or 0 %.

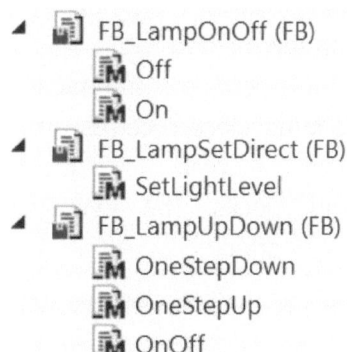

These three function blocks are controlled by `FB_Controller`. An instance of each lamp type is instantiated in `FB_Controller`. The desired lamp is selected via the property `eActiveLamp` of type `E_LampType`:

```
TYPE E_LampType :
(
   Unknown       := -1,
   SetDirect     :=  0,
   OnOff         :=  1,
   UpDown        :=  2
) := Unknown;
END_TYPE
```

In turn, `FB_Controller` has appropriate methods for controlling the different lamp types. The `DimDown()` and `DimUp()` methods dim the selected lamp by 5 % upwards or 5 % downwards. While the `On()` and `Off()` methods switch the lamp on or off directly.

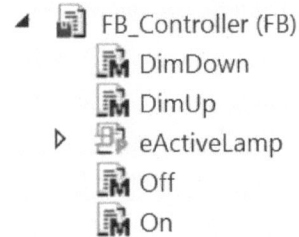

The *Observer Pattern* [1] is used to transmit the output variable between the controller and the selected lamp. The controller contains an instance of `FB_AnalogValue` for this purpose. `FB_AnalogValue` implements the interface `I_Observer` with the method `Update()`, while the three function blocks for the lamps implement the interface `I_Subject`. Using the `Attach()` method, each lamp block receives an interface pointer to the `I_Observer` interface of `FB_AnalogValue`. If the output value changes in one of the three lamp blocks, the new value is transferred to `FB_AnalogValue` from the interface `I_Observer` via the method `Update()`.

Our example so far consists of the following actors:

---

[1] https://StefanHenneken.net/2018/05/27/iec-61131-3-the-observer-pattern

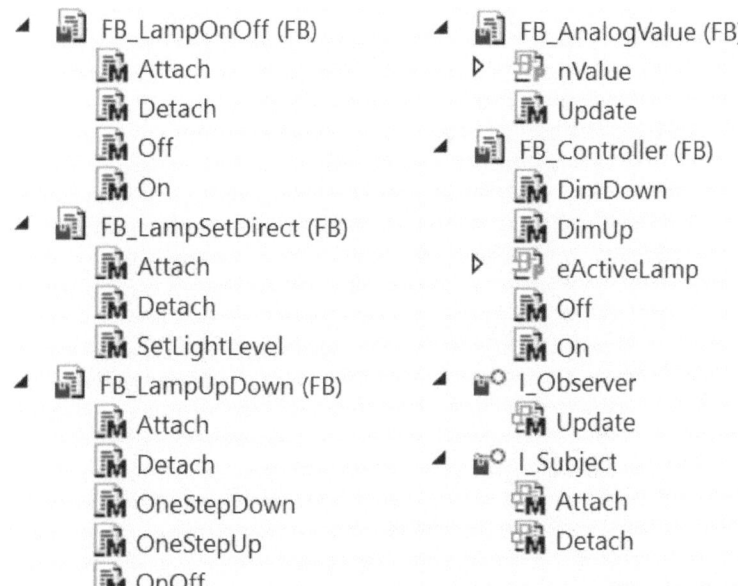

The UML diagram shows the relationships between the respective elements:

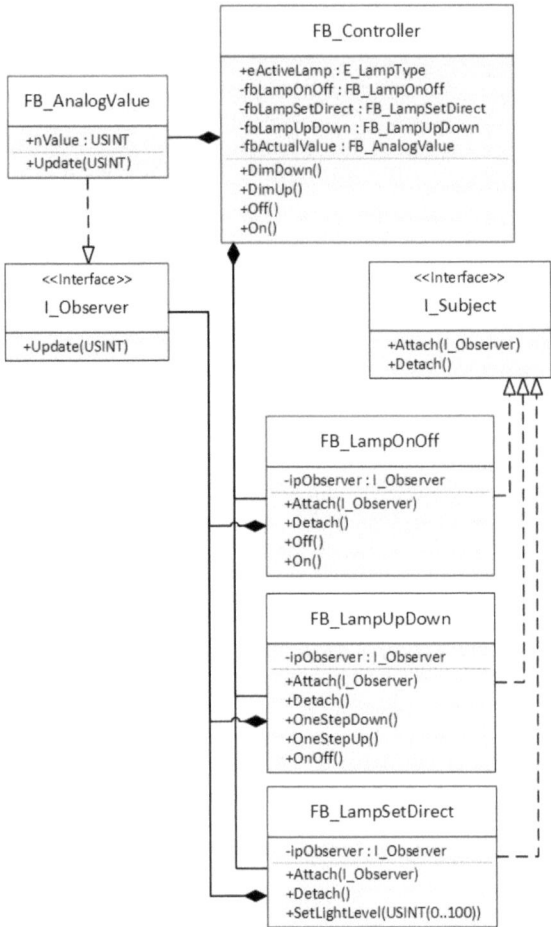

Let's take a closer look at the program code of the individual function blocks.

4.1.1   FB_LampOnOff / FB_LampUpDown / FB_LampSetDirect

`FB_LampSetDirect` is used here as an example for the three lamp types. `FB_LampSetDirect` has a local variable for the current output value and a local variable for the interface pointer to `FB_AnalogValue`:

```
FUNCTION_BLOCK PUBLIC FB_LampSetDirect IMPLEMENTS I_Subject
VAR
   nLightLevel : USINT;
```

```
  _ipObserver : I_Observer;
END_VAR
```

If `FB_Controller` switches to the lamp of the type `FB_LampSetDirect`, `FB_Controller` calls the `Attach()` method and passes the interface pointer to `FB_AnalogValue` to `FB_LampSetDirect`. If the value is valid (not equal to 0), it is saved in the local variable (backing variable) `_ipObserver`.

Note: Local variables that store the value of a property are also known as backing variables and are indicated by an underscore in the variable name.

```
METHOD Attach
VAR_INPUT
  ipObserver : I_Observer;
END_VAR
IF (ipObserver = 0) THEN
  RETURN;
END_IF
_ipObserver := ipObserver;
```

The `Detach()` method sets the interface pointer to 0, which means that the `Update()` method is no longer called (see below):

```
METHOD Detach
_ipObserver := 0;
```

The new output value is passed via the `SetLightLevel()` method and stored in the local variable `nLightLevel`. In addition, the method `Update()` is called by the interface pointer `_ipObserver`. This gives the new output value to the instance of `FB_AnalogValue` located in `FB_Controller`:

```
METHOD PUBLIC SetLightLevel
VAR_INPUT
  nNewLightLevel : USINT(0..100);
END_VAR
nLightLevel := nNewLightLevel;
IF (_ipObserver <> 0) THEN
  _ipObserver.Update(nLightLevel);
END_IF
```

The `Attach()` and `Detach()` methods are identical for all three lamp blocks. There are differences only in the methods that change the initial value.

4.1.2   FB_AnalogValue

`FB_AnalogValue` contains very little program code, since this function block is only used to store the output variable:

```
FUNCTION_BLOCK PUBLIC FB_AnalogValue IMPLEMENTS I_Observer
VAR
   _nActualValue : USINT;
END_VAR

METHOD Update : USINT
VAR_INPUT
   nNewValue : USINT;
END_VAR
```

In addition, `FB_AnalogValue` has the property nValue, via which the current value is made available externally.

4.1.3   FB_Controller

`FB_Controller` contains the instances of the three lamp blocks. Furthermore, there is an instance of `FB_AnalogValue` to receive the current output value of the active lamp. `_eActiveLamp` stores the current state of the `eActiveLamp` property:

```
FUNCTION_BLOCK PUBLIC FB_Controller
VAR
   fbLampOnOff        : FB_LampOnOff();
   fbLampSetDirect    : FB_LampSetDirect();
   fbLampUpDown       : FB_LampUpDown();
   fbActualValue      : FB_AnalogValue();
   _eActiveLamp       : E_LampType;
END_VAR
```

Switching between the three lamps is done by the setter of the `eActiveLamp` property:

```
Off();

fbLampOnOff.Detach();
fbLampSetDirect.Detach();
fbLampUpDown.Detach();

CASE eActiveLamp OF
   E_LampType.OnOff:
```

```
    fbLampOnOff.Attach(fbActualValue);
  E_LampType.SetDirect:
    fbLampSetDirect.Attach(fbActualValue);
  E_LampType.UpDown:
    fbLampUpDown.Attach(fbActualValue);
END_CASE

_eActiveLamp := eActiveLamp;
```

If the `eActiveLamp` property is used to switch to another lamp, the current lamp is switched off at first using the local method `Off()`. Furthermore, the method `Detach()` is called for all three lamps. This terminates a possible connection to `FB_AnalogValue`. Within the CASE statement, the method `Attach()` is called for the new lamp and the interface pointer is passed to `fbActualValue`. Finally, the state of the property is saved in the local variable `_eActiveLamp`.

The methods `DimDown()`, `DimUp()`, `Off()` and `On()` have the task of setting the desired output value. Since the individual lamp types offer different methods for this, each lamp type must be handled individually.

The `DimDown()` method should dim the active lamp by 5 %. However, the initial value should not fall below 10 %:

```
METHOD PUBLIC DimDown
CASE _eActiveLamp OF
  E_LampType.OnOff:
    fbLampOnOff.Off();
  E_LampType.SetDirect:
    IF (fbActualValue.nValue >= 15) THEN
      fbLampSetDirect.SetLightLevel(
                                fbActualValue.nValue - 5);
    END_IF
  E_LampType.UpDown:
    IF (fbActualValue.nValue >= 15) THEN
      fbLampUpDown.OneStepDown();
      fbLampUpDown.OneStepDown();
      fbLampUpDown.OneStepDown();
      fbLampUpDown.OneStepDown();
      fbLampUpDown.OneStepDown();
    END_IF
END_CASE
```

`FB_LampOnOff` only knows the states 0 % and 100 %. Dimming is therefore not possible. As a compromise, the lamp will in fact be switched off when it is dimmed down (line 4).

With `FB_LampSetDirect`, the `SetLightLevel()` method can be used to set the new initial value directly. To do this, 5 is subtracted from the current output value and passed to the `SetLightLevel()` method (line 7). The IF query in line 6 ensures that the initial value is not set below 10 %.

Since the `OneStepDown()` method of `FB_LampUpDown` only reduces the initial value by 1 %, the method is called 5 times (lines 11-15). Here again, the IF query in line 10 ensures that the value does not fall below 10 %. `DimUp()`, `Off()` and `On()` have a comparable structure. The various lamp types are treated separately using a CASE statement, and the respective special features are thus taken into account.

The example is available for download for TwinCAT 3.1 on GitHub[2].

4.2   Implementation analysis

At first glance, the implementation seems solid. The program does what it should and the presented code is maintainable in its current size. If it were ensured that the program would not increase in size, everything could remain as it is.

But in practice, the current state is more like the first development cycle of a larger project. The small manageable application will grow in code size over time as extensions are added. Thus, a close inspection of the code right at the beginning makes sense. Otherwise, there is a risk of missing the right time for fundamental optimizations. Defects can then only be eliminated with a great deal of time.

But what are the fundamental issues with the above example?

---

[2] https://github.com/StefanHenneken/Blog-2021-05-IEC61131-DIP-Sample01

4.2.1 1ˢᵗ issue: CASE statement

Every method of the controller has the same CASE construct:

```
CASE _eActiveLamp OF
  E_LampType.OnOff:
    fbLampOnOff...
  E_LampType.SetDirect:
    fbLampSetDirect...
  E_LampType.UpDown:
    fbLampUpDown...
END_CASE
```

Although there is a similarity between the value of `_eActiveLamp` (e.g., `E_LampType.SetDirect`) and the local variable (e.g., `fbLampSetDirect`), the individual cases have still to be observed and programmed manually.

4.2.2 2ⁿᵈ issue: Extensibility

If a new lamp type has to be added, the data type `E_LampType` must first be extended. Then, it is necessary to add the CASE statement in each method of the controller.

4.2.3 3ʳᵈ issue: Responsibilities

Because the controller assigns the commands to all lamp types, the logic of a lamp type is distributed over several FBs. This is an extremely impractical grouping. If you want to understand how the controller addresses a specific lamp type, you have to jump from method to method and pick the correct case in the CASE statement.

4.2.4 4ᵗʰ issue: Coupling

The controller has a close connection to the different lamp modules. As a result, the controller is highly dependent on changes to the individual lamp types. Every change to the methods of a lamp type inevitably leads to adjustments of the controller.

4.3 Optimizing of the implementation

Currently, the example has fixed dependencies in one direction. The controller calls the methods of the respective lamp types. This direct dependency should be resolved. To do this, we need a common level of abstraction.

4.3.1 Resolving the CASE statements

Abstract function blocks and interfaces can be used for this purpose. In the following, I use the abstract function block `FB_Lamp` and the interface `I_Lamp`. The interface `I_Lamp` has the same methods as the controller. The abstract FB implements the interface `I_Lamp` and thus also has all the methods of `FB_Controller`.

I presented in *IEC 61131-3: Abstract FB vs. Interface* [3], how abstract function blocks and interfaces can be combined with each other.

All lamp types inherit from this abstract lamp type. This makes all lamp types look the same from the controller's point of view. Furthermore, the abstract FB implements the `I_Subject` interface:

```
FUNCTION_BLOCK PUBLIC ABSTRACT FB_Lamp IMPLEMENTS I_Subject,
I_Lamp
```

The methods `Detach()` and `Attach()` of `FB_Lamp` are not declared as abstract and contain the necessary program code. This means that it is not necessary to implement the program code for these two methods in each lamp type again.

---

[3] https://StefanHenneken.net/2020/12/13/iec-61131-3-abstract-fb-vs-interface

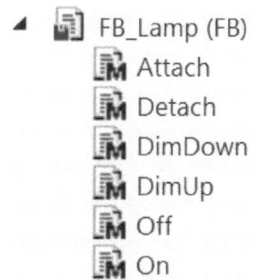

Since the lamp types inherit from `FB_Lamp`, they are all the same from the controller's point of view.

The `SetLightLevel()` method remains unchanged. The assignment of the methods of `FB_Lamp` (`DimDown()`, `DimUp()`, `Off()` and `On()`) to the individual lamp types is now no longer done in the controller, but in the respective FB of the lamp type:

```
METHOD PUBLIC DimDown
IF (nLightLevel >= 15) THEN
   SetLightLevel(nLightLevel - 5);
END_IF
```

Thus, the controller is no longer responsible for assigning the methods, but rather each lamp type itself. The CASE statements in the `FB_Controller` methods are omitted completely.

4.3.2 Resolving E_LampType

The use of `E_LampType` still binds the controller to the respective lamp types. But how to switch to the different lamp types if `E_LampType` is omitted? To achieve this, the desired lamp type is passed to the controller via a property by reference:

```
PROPERTY PUBLIC refActiveLamp : REFERENCE TO FB_Lamp
```

Thus, all lamp types can be passed. The only condition is that the passed lamp type must inherit from FB_Lamp. This defines all methods and properties that are necessary for an interaction between the controller and the lamp block.

Note: This technique of „injecting" dependencies is also called *Dependency Injection* [4].

Switching to the new lamp module is done in the setter of the refActiveLamp property. The method Detach() of the active lamp is called there (line 2), while the method Attach() is called in line 6 by the new lamp. In line 4, the reference of the new lamp is stored in the local variable (backing variable) _refActiveLamp:

```
IF (__ISVALIDREF(_refActiveLamp)) THEN
   _refActiveLamp.Detach();
END_IF
_refActiveLamp REF= refActiveLamp;
IF (__ISVALIDREF(refActiveLamp)) THEN
   refActiveLamp.Attach(fbActualValue);
END_IF
```

In the methods DimDown(), DimUp(), Off() and On(), the method call is forwarded to the active lamp via _refActiveLamp. Instead of the CASE statement, there are only a few lines here, since it is no longer necessary to distinguish between the different lamp types:

```
METHOD PUBLIC DimDown
IF (__ISVALIDREF(_refActiveLamp)) THEN
   _refActiveLamp.DimDown();
END_IF
```

The controller is therefore generic. If a new lamp type is defined, the controller remains unchanged.

---

[4] https://en.wikipedia.org/wiki/Dependency_injection

Note: This delegated the task of selecting the desired lamp type to the caller of `FB_Controller`. Now, it must create the various lamp types and pass them to the controller. This is a good approach if, for example, all elements are contained in a library. With the adjustments shown above, it is now possible to develop your own lamp types without having to make adjustments to the library.

The example is available for download for TwinCAT 3.1 on GitHub[5].

4.4   Optimization analysis

Although a function block and an interface have been added, the amount of program code has not increased. The code only needed to be reasonably restructured to eliminate the problems mentioned above. The result is a long-term sustainable program structure, which was divided into several consistently small artifacts with clear responsibilities. The UML diagram shows the new distribution very well:

---

[5] https://github.com/StefanHenneken/Blog-2021-05-IEC61131-DIP-Sample02

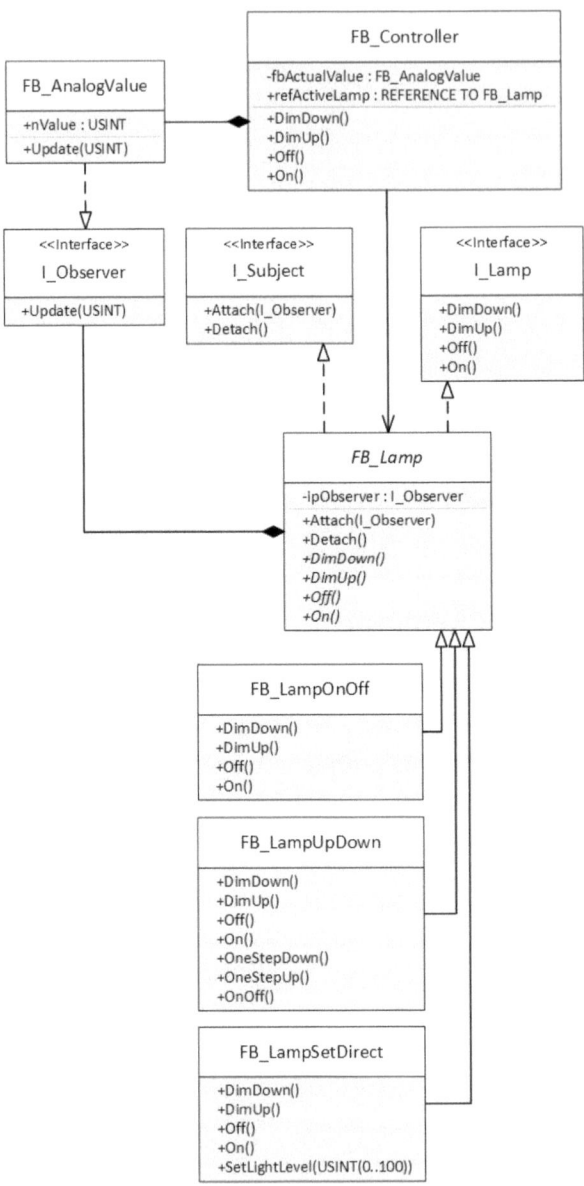

FB_Controller no longer has a fixed binding to the individual lamp types. Instead, the abstract function block FB_Lamp is accessed, which is passed to the controller via the refActiveLamp property. The individual lamp types are then accessed via this abstraction level.

4.5 The definition of the Dependency Inversion Principle

The *Dependency Inversion Principle* consists of two rules and is described very well in the book *Clean Architecture: A Craftsman's Guide to Software Structure and Design* by Robert C. Martin:

> *High-level modules should not depend on low-level modules. Both should depend on abstractions.*

Referring to the above example, the high-level module is the `FB_Controller` function block. It should not directly access low-level modules that contain details. The low-level modules are the individual lamp types.

> *Abstractions should not depend on details. Details should depend on abstractions.*

The details are the individual methods offered by the respective lamp types. In the first example, `FB_Controller` depends on the details of all lamp types. If a change is made to a lamp type, the controller must also be adapted.

What exactly does the *Dependency Inversion Principle* invert?

In the first example, `FB_Controller` accesses the individual lamp types directly. This makes `FB_Controller` (higher level) dependent on the lamp types (lower level).

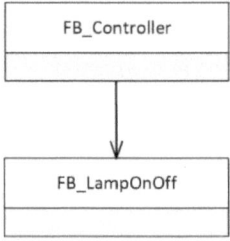

The *Dependency Inversion Principle* inverts this dependency. For this purpose, an additional abstraction level is introduced. The higher layer specifies what this abstraction layer looks like. The lower layers must meet these requirements. This changes the direction of the dependencies.

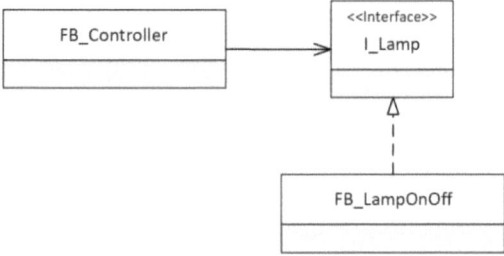

In the above example, this additional abstraction level was implemented by combining the abstract function block FB_Lamp and the interface I_Lamp.

4.6 Summary

With the *Dependency Inversion Principle*, there is a risk of overengineering. Not every coupling should be resolved. Where an exchange of function blocks is to be expected, the *Dependency Inversion Principle* can be of great help. Above, I gave an example of a library in which different function blocks are interdependent. If the user of the library wants to intervene in these dependencies, fixed dependencies would prevent this.

The *Dependency Inversion Principle* increases the testability of a system. FB_Controller can be tested completely independently of the individual lamp types. For the unit tests, an FB is created which is derived from

`FB_Lamp`. This dummy FB contains only functions that are necessary for the tests of `FB_Controller`, and is also called a mocking object. Jakob Sagatowski introduces this concept in his post *Mocking objects in TwinCAT*[6].

---

[6] https://alltwincat.com/2018/05/23/mocking-objects-in-twincat

5   The Single Responsibility Principle

The *Single Responsibility Principle* is one of the more important of the SOLID principles. It is responsible for decomposition of modules and encapsulates the idea that each unit of code should be responsible for just a single, clearly defined role. This ensures that software remains extensible long term and makes it easier to maintain.

To illustrate the *Single Responsibility Principle* concept, I'm going to use the example from the chapter. That chapter showed how to use the *Dependency Inversion Principle* to eliminate fixed dependencies.

5.1   Starting situation

There are three different lamp types, with a corresponding function block for each (`FB_LampOnOff`, `FB_LampSetDirect` and `FB_LampUpDown`). Each lamp type works in a different way and provides appropriate methods for modifying the output value.

A higher-level controller (`FB_Controller`) provides access to a single application programming interface (API) for addressing the three lamp types. The *Dependency Inversion Principle* is applied to avoid having a fixed dependency between the controller and lamp types. The unitary API is defined by `I_Lamp`. The `I_Lamp` interface is implemented by the abstract function block `FB_Lamp`. `FB_Lamp` contains identical program code for all three lamp types. Having all lamp types derived from `FB_Lamp` means that the controller and lamps are decoupled. Instead of creating instances of specific lamp types, the controller manages just a single reference to `FB_Lamp`.

5.2   Implementation analysis

We're going to use the function block `FB_LampUpDown` to evaluate the implementation in more detail. At the beginning of this series of articles, this function block contained only three methods for changing the output value: `OneStepDown()`, `OneStepUp()` and `OnOff()`.

5.2.1 1st issue: multiple roles

In applying the *Dependency Inversion Principle*, we added the methods `DimDown()`, `DimUp()`, `Off()` and `On()` via the `FB_Lamp` abstract function block and the `I_Lamp` interface. These four methods represent an „adapter" between `FB_Controller` and the concrete `FB_LampUpDown` implementation.

The UML diagram below shows the two roles the `FB_LampUpDown` component currently performs. The methods inherited from `FB_Lamp` are marked in blue (role as adapter for `FB_Controller`). The area marked in green indicates the actual role performed by this function block (role as `FB_LampUpDown`).

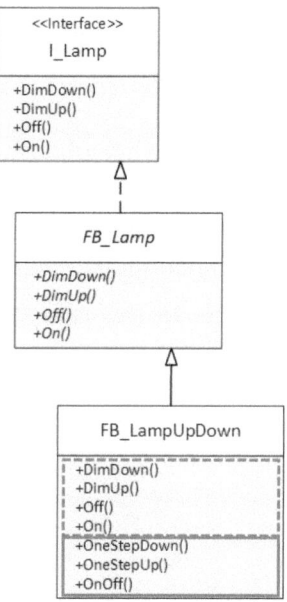

At this point, we might consider designating the `OneStepDown()`, `OneStepUp()` and `OnOff()` methods as PRIVATE. We can only do this, however, if `FB_LampUpDown` has not previously been used in any other context. Otherwise, every extension would need to ensure that the function block retained backwards compatibility.

5.3 Optimizing of the implementation

As was the case in our demonstration of the *Dependency Inversion Principle*, the program as it stands is very maintainable. But what happens if we add additional roles? A future development cycle might, for example, need to implement additional adapters. The actual `FB_LampUpDown` logic would be lost in the adapter implementation.

5.3.1 Creating the adapter

We therefore need a tool to separate the individual roles. Ideally a tool that ensures that the original implementation of `FB_LampUpDown` remains unchanged. This will also be necessary if, for example, `FB_LampUpDown` resides in a PLC library and is therefore outside the developer's control.

5.3.1.1 Approch 1: inheritance

One possible solution would be to use inheritance. The new adapter function block (`FB_LampUpDownAdapter`) inherits from `FB_LampUpDown`. But it would also have to inherit from `FB_Lamp`. Since multiple inheritance is, however, not permitted, one option would be to have `FB_LampUpDownAdapter` implement the `I_Lamp` interface. In this case, the abstract function block `FB_Lamp` is rendered redundant.

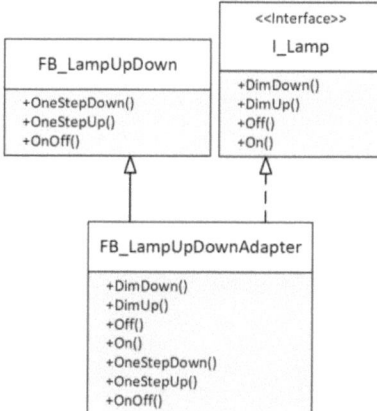

By inheriting from FB_LampUpDown, the adapter also provides external access to methods that are not required for interaction with the controller. With this approach, therefore, FB_LampUpDownAdapter exposes details of the FB_LampUpDown implementation.

5.3.1.2 Approch 2: adapter pattern

In this case, the adapter contains an internal instance of FB_LampUpDown. The methods involved in adapter function are simply passed internally to FB_LampUpDown. This approach avoids exposing details of FB_LampUpDown externally.

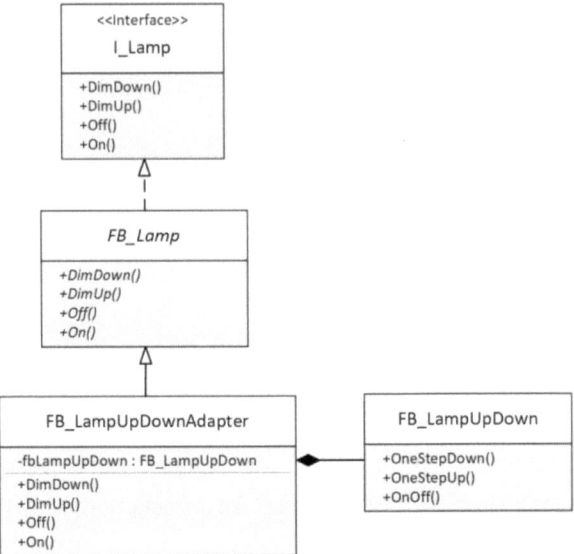

This approach meets our objective of clearly separating the role of the adapter from the lamp logic. The lamp implementation does not need to be modified.

The example is available for download for TwinCAT 3.1 on GitHub[7].

5.4 Optimization analysis

Let's take a closer look at the program after implementing the *Single Responsibility Principle*.

---

[7] https://github.com/StefanHenneken/Blog-2022-02-IEC61131-SRP-Sample01

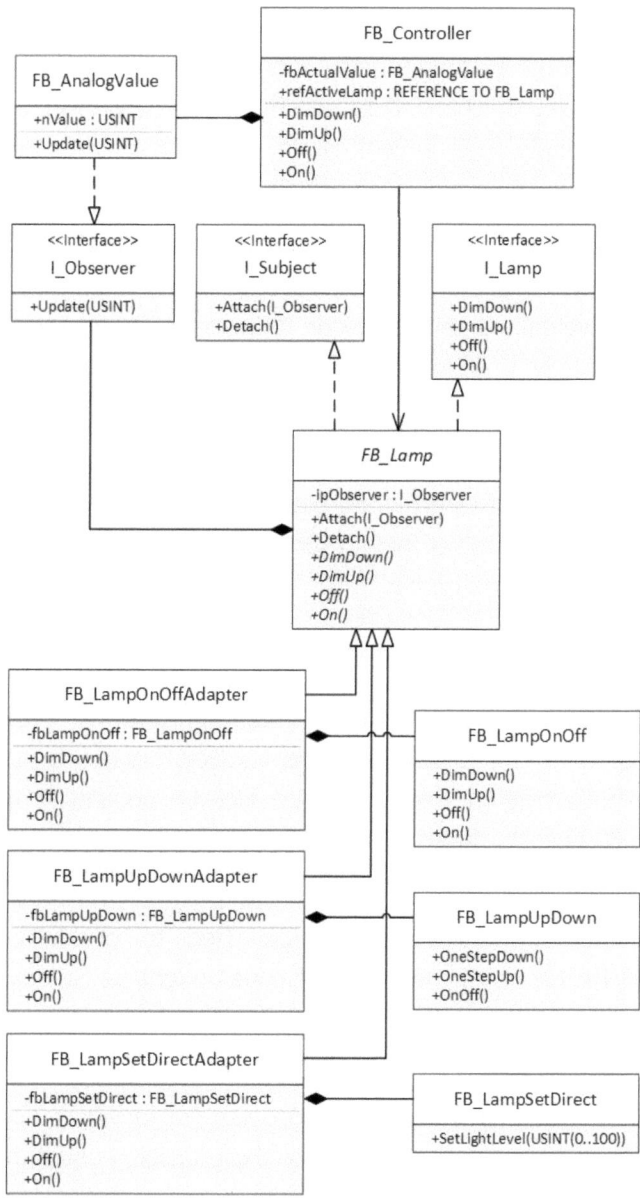

Responsibilities are now clearly separated. If we need to extend the program code, it's easy to work out which function block we need to modify.

If we need to add additional adapters, there is no need to extend the implementation of the existing function blocks for the lamps. We don't need to worry about these function blocks becoming more and more bloated over the course of multiple development cycles.

Separating independent roles into individual, independent units of code (function blocks) makes the program easier to maintain. But it also means more function blocks, making it harder to grasp the overall picture. Consequently, we should not be looking to increase the number of function blocks unnecessarily. Creating individual function blocks for individual roles is not always desirable.

Since program functionality is always expanding, function blocks should be split up when they start to grow too big. SOLID principles can help you in implementing this. This raises the question, however, of how we judge when a unit of code has grown too big.

5.5   Class Responsibility Collaboration (CRC)

Counting the lines of code is not a good approach to evaluating the complexity of a unit of code. Code metrics like this can be useful tools (worthy of an article in itself), but I'd like to present a method for determining complexity based on the requirements of a unit of code.

The use of the term „unit of code", rather than „function block", is deliberate. This approach can also be used to evaluate a system architecture. In this case, the „units of code" might be, for example, the individual services. This method is not confined to evaluating pure source code alone.

The method I'm going to look at is called *Class Responsibility Collaboration.* The name gives a pretty good insight into the principle behind this method:

- We start by listing all of the function blocks (**class**).

- We then write down the role or **responsibility** of each function block.

- We then note down which other function blocks each function block **collaborates** with.

The CRC method flags up very clearly any imbalances in a software system. Responsibilities and dependencies should be evenly distributed across all function blocks.

To create CRC cards, I use *SimpleCrcTool* [8], wich can be run directly in a browser[9]. To keep things simple, our analysis will ignore the function block `FB_AnalogValue`. In all variants of our sample program, this operates in the same way to transfer the output value between the relevant lamp type and the controller.

5.5.1 Step 1: Initial state

We will start by analysing the program in its original form, i.e. before we undertook any optimisation (see Chapter: *The Dependency Inversion Principle*).

---

[8] https://github.com/guidolx/simple-crc-app
[9] https://guidolx.github.io/simple-crc-app

FB_Controller
FB_LampOnOff, FB_LampSetDirect, FB_LampUpDown
- Switching between the different types of lamps - Adapting the On command to the selected lamp type - Adapting the Off command to the selected lamp type - Adapting the DimUp command to the selected lamp type - Adapting the DimDown command to the selected   lamp type

FB_LampOnOff	**FB_LampSetDirect**	**FB_LampUpDown**
- Internal logic of the OnOff lamp type	- Internal logic of the SetDirect lamp type	- Internal logic of the UpDown lamp type

We can clearly see that the controller performs a very large number of roles, but the functionality of each lamp type is easily understood. It's a similar story with dependencies. The controller addresses each lamp type directly.

5.5.2 Step 2: Applying the Dependency Inversion Principle

By applying the *Dependency Inversion Principle*, we eliminate fixed dependencies between the controller and lamp types. Now, the controller only addresses the abstract function block `FB_Lamp`, and no longer addresses each lamp type.

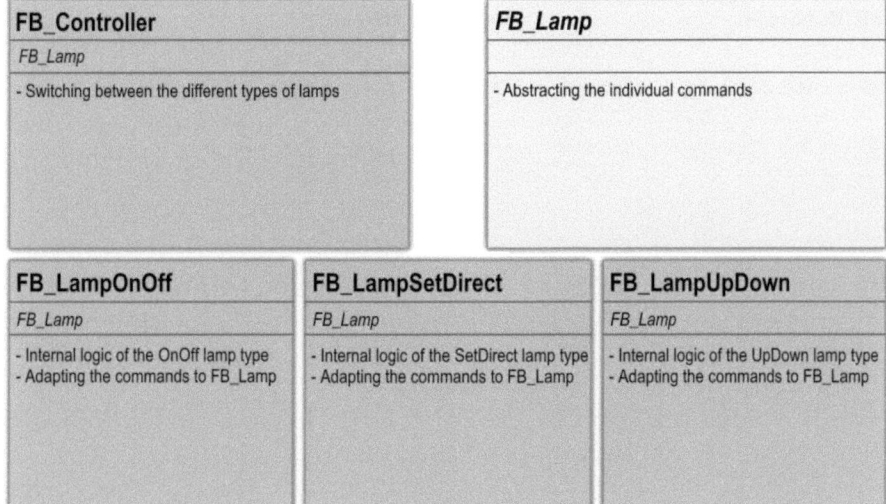

The disadvantage with this setup is that each lamp type performs more than one role – the logic for the specific lamp type and mapping to the abstract lamp.

5.5.3 Step 3: Applying the Single Responsibility Principle

To bring this setup in line with the *Single Responsibility Principle*, we use the *Adapter Pattern*. Each lamp type now has an adapter function block responsible for mapping between the abstract lamp and the specific lamp type.

FB_Controller	FB_Lamp
FB_Lamp	
- Switching between the different types of lamps	- Abstracting the individual commands

FB_LampOnOffAdapter	FB_LampSetDirectAdapter	FB_LampUpDownAdapter
FB_Lamp, FB_LampOnOff	*FB_Lamp, FB_LampSetDirect*	*FB_Lamp, FB_LampUpDown*
- Adapting the commands to FB_Lamp	- Adapting the commands to FB_Lamp	- Adapting the commands to FB_Lamp

FB_LampOnOff	FB_LampSetDirect	FB_LampUpDown
- Internal logic of the OnOff lamp type	- Internal logic of the SetDirect lamp type	- Internal logic of the UpDown lamp type

After optimisation, each function block performs just a single role. We now have a large number of small, rather than a small number of large function blocks.

5.6 The Definition of the Single Responsibility Principle

Now let's take a look at the definition of the *Single Responsibility Principle*. The principle was defined in the book *Clean Architecture: A Craftsman's Guide to Software Structure and Design* by Robert C. Martin back in the early 2000s as:

> *A class should have only one reason to change.*

Robert C. Martin has also expressed this as:

> *A module should be responsible to one, and only one, actor.*

But what does module mean in this context and who or what is an actor?

A **module** in this context is a unit of code. What a module is depends on the angle from which you're looking at the software system. From the point of view of a software architect, a module might be a REST service, a communication channel or a database system. For a software developer, a module might be a function block or an interrelated set of function blocks and functions. In the above example, the modules were function blocks.

Similarly, the term **actor** does not necessarily represent a person; it can also refer to a specific set of users or stakeholders.

5.7 Summary

In the previous chapter, we applied the *Dependency Inversion Principle* to decouple the controller (`FB_Controller`) from the individual lamps. This also required modifications to the individual lamp function blocks. The *Single Responsibility Principle* was then used to further optimise this decoupling.

Is it good practice if a single function block is responsible for compressing and encrypting data? No! Compression and encryption are completely different responsibilities. You can compress data without worrying about encryption. Similarly, encryption is independent of compression. They are completely independent roles. If compression and encryption were dealt with within the same function block, there would be two reasons to change – encryption and compression.

A further example of the *Single Responsibility Principle* in action (from a software architecture perspective) is the ISO/OSI model for network protocols. The model defines seven sequential layers, each performing clearly defined roles. This makes it possible to replace individual layers without affecting higher or lower layers. Each layer has one(!) single clearly defined role, e.g. transmission of raw bits.

6 The Liskov Substitution Principle

„The *Liskov Substitution Principle* requires that derived function blocks (FBs) are always compatible to their base FB. Derived FBs must behave like their respective base FB. A derived FB may extend the base FB, but not restrict it." This is the core statement of the *Liskov Substitution Principle*, which Barbara Liskov formulated already in the late 1980s. Although the *Liskov Substitution Principle* is one of the simpler SOLID principles, its violation is very common. The following example shows why the *Liskov Substitution Principle* is important.

6.1 Starting situation

Again, the example is used, which was already developed and optimized in the two previous chapters. The core of the example are three lamp types, which are mapped by the function blocks `FB_LampOnOff`, `FB_LampSetDirect` and `FB_LampUpDown`. The interface `I_Lamp` and the abstract function block `FB_Lamp` secure a clear decoupling between the respective lamp types and the higher-level controller `FB_Controller`.

FB_Controller no longer accesses specific instances, but only a reference of the abstract function block FB_Lamp. The Dependency Inversion Principle is used to break the fixed coupling.

To realize the required functionality, each lamp type provides its own methods. For this reason, each lamp type also has a corresponding adapter function block (`FB_LampOnOffAdapter`, `FB_LampSetDirectAdapter` and `FB_LampUpDownAdapter`), which is responsible for mapping between the abstract lamp (`FB_Lamp`) and the concrete lamp types (`FB_LampOnOff`, `FB_LampSetDirect` and `FB_LampUpDown`). This optimization is supported by the *Single Responsibility Principle*.

6.2 Extension of the implementation

The three required lamp types can be mapped well by the existing software design. Nevertheless, it can happen that extensions, which seem simple at first sight, lead to difficulties later. The new lamp type `FB_LampSetDirectDALI` will serve as an example here.

DALI stands for *Digital Addressable Lighting Interface* [10] and is a protocol for controlling lighting devices. Basically, the new function block behaves like `FB_LampSetDirect`, but with DALI the output value is not given in 0-100 % but in 0-254.

6.3 Optimization and analysis of the extensions

Which approaches are available to implement this extension? The different approaches will also be analyzed in more detail.

6.3.1 Approach 1: Quick & Dirty

High time pressure can tempt to realize the Quick & Dirty implementation. Since `FB_LampSetDirect` behaves similarly to the new DALI lamp type, `FB_LampSetDirectDALI` inherits from `FB_LampSetDirect`. To enable the value range of 0-254, the `SetLightLevel()` method of `FB_LampSetDirectDALI` is overwritten:

```
METHOD PUBLIC SetLightLevel
VAR_INPUT
  nNewLightLevel : USINT(0..254);
END_VAR
nLightLevel := nNewLightLevel;
```

The new adapter function block (`FB_LampSetDirectDALIAdapter`) is also adapted so that the methods regard the value range 0-254.

As an example, the methods `DimUp()` and `On()` are shown here:

```
METHOD PUBLIC DimUp
IF (fbLampSetDirectDALI.nLightLevel <= 249) THEN
```

---

[10] https://www.dali-alliance.org

```
     fbLampSetDirectDALI.SetLightLevel(
                          fbLampSetDirectDALI.nLightLevel + 5);
END_IF
IF (_ipObserver <> 0) THEN
  _ipObserver.Update(fbLampSetDirectDALI.nLightLevel);
END_IF

METHOD PUBLIC On
fbLampSetDirectDALI.SetLightLevel(254);
IF (_ipObserver <> 0) THEN
  _ipObserver.Update(fbLampSetDirectDALI.nLightLevel);
END_IF
```

The simplified UML diagram shows the integration of the function blocks for the DALI lamp into the existing software design:

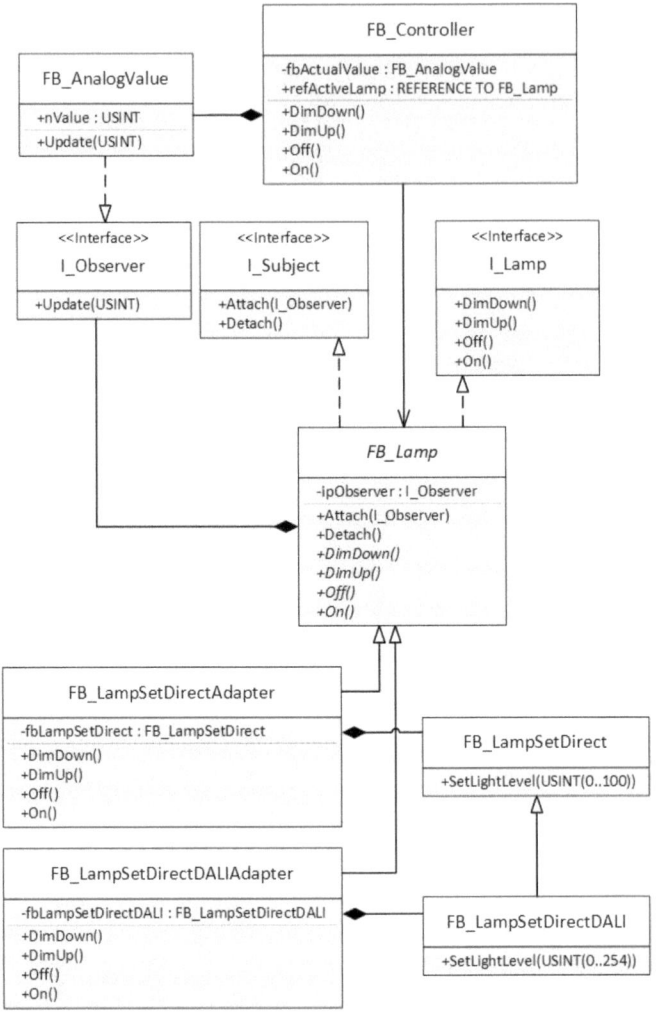

The example is available for download for TwinCAT 3.1 on GitHub[11].

This approach implements the requirements quickly and easily through a pragmatic strategy. But this also added some specifics that complicate the use of the blocks in an application.

---

[11] https://github.com/StefanHenneken/Blog-2022-04-IEC61131-LSP-Sample01

For example, how should a user interface behave when it connects to an instance of `FB_Controller` and `FB_AnalogValue` outputs a value of 100? Does 100 mean that the current lamp is at 100 % or does the new DALI lamp output a value of 100, which would be well below 100 %?

The user of `FB_Controller` must always know the active lamp type in order to interpret the current output value correctly. `FB_LampSetDirectDALI` inherits from `FB_LampSetDirect`, but changes its behavior. In this example, the behavior is changed by overwriting the `SetLightLevel()` method. The derived FB (`FB_LampSetDirectDALI`) behaves differently to the base FB (`FB_LampSetDirect`). `FB_LampSetDirect` can no longer be replaced (substituted) by `FB_LampSetDirectDALI`. The *Liskov Substitution Principle* is violated.

6.3.2 Approach 2: Optionality

In this approach, each lamp type contains a property that returns information about the exact function of the function block.

In .NET, for example, this approach is used in the abstract class `System.IO.Stream`. The `Stream` class serves as the base class for specialized streams (e.g., `FileStream` and `NetworkStream`) and specifies the most important methods and properties. This includes the methods `Write()`, `Read()` and `Seek()`. Since not every stream can provide all functions, the properties `CanRead`, `CanWrite` and `CanSeek` provide information about whether the corresponding method is supported by the respective stream. For example, `NetworkStream` can check at runtime whether writing to the stream is possible or whether it is a read-only stream.

In our example, `I_Lamp` is extended by the property `bIsDALIDevice`.

This means that `FB_Lamp` and therefore every adapter function block also receives this property. Since the functionality of `bIsDALIDevice` is the same in all adapter function blocks, `bIsDALIDevice` is not declared as abstract in `FB_Lamp`. This means that it is not necessary for all adapter function blocks to implement this property themselves. The functionality of `bIsDALIDevice` is inherited by `FB_Lamp` to all adapter function blocks.

For `FB_LampSetDirectDALIAdapter`, the backing variable of the property `bIsDALIDevice` is set to `TRUE` in the method `FB_init()`:

```
METHOD FB_init : BOOL
VAR_INPUT
  bInitRetains : BOOL;
  bInCopyCode  : BOOL;
END_VAR
SUPER^._bIsDALIDevice := TRUE;
```

For all other adapter function blocks, `_bIsDALIDevice` retains its initialization value (`FALSE`). The use of the `FB_init()` method is not necessary for these adapter function blocks.

The user of `FB_Controller` (`MAIN` block) can now query at program runtime whether the current lamp is a DALI lamp or not. If this is the case, the output value is scaled accordingly to 0-100 %:

```
IF (__ISVALIDREF(fbController.refActiveLamp) AND_THEN
    fbController.refActiveLamp.bIsDALIDevice) THEN
  nLightLevel := TO_USINT(fbController.fbActualValue.nValue
                                     * 100.0 / 254.0);
ELSE
  nLightLevel := fbController.fbActualValue.nValue;
END_IF
```

Note: It is important to use the `AND_THEN` operator instead of `THEN`. This means that the expression to the right of `AND_THEN` is only executed if the first operand (to the left of `AND_THEN`) is `TRUE`. This is important here because otherwise the expression `fbController.refActiveLamp.bIsDALIDevice` would terminate the execution of the program in case of an invalid reference to the active lamp (refActiveLamp).

The UML diagram shows how `FB_Lamp` receives the property `bIsDALIDevice` via the interface `I_Lamp` and is thus inherited by all adapter function blocks:

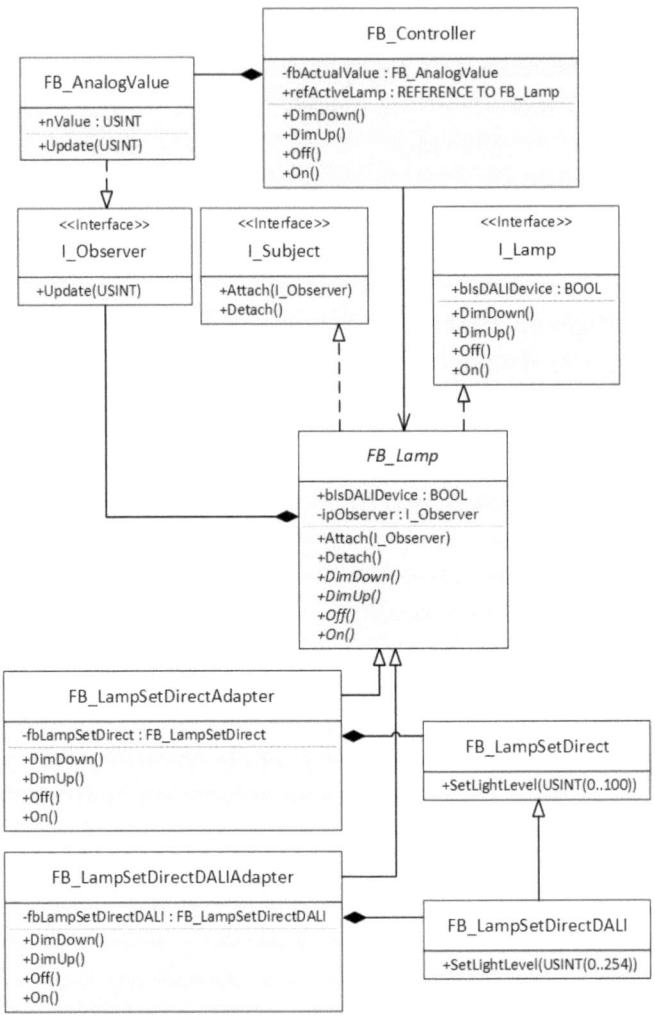

The example is available for download for TwinCAT 3.1 on GitHub[12].

This approach still violates the *Liskov Substitution Principle*. FB_LampSetDirectDALI behaves further on differently to FB_LampSetDirect. The user hast to take this difference into account

---

[12] https://github.com/StefanHenneken/Blog-2022-04-IEC61131-LSP-Sample02

(querying `bIsDALIDevice`) and correct it (scaling to 0-100 %). This is easy to overlook or to implement incorrectly.

6.3.3 Approach 3: Harmonization

In order not to violate the *Liskov Substitution Principle* any further, the inheritance between `FB_LampSetDirect` and `FB_LampSetDirectDALI` is resolved. Even if both function blocks appear very similar at first glance, the inheritance should be avoided with at this point.

The adapter function blocks ensure that all lamp types can be controlled using the same methods. However, there are still differences in the representation of the output value.

In `FB_Controller` the initial value of the active lamp is represented by an instance of `FB_AnalogValue`. A new initial value is transmitted by the `Update()` method. To ensure that the initial value is also displayed uniformly, it is scaled to 0-100 % before the `Update()` method is called. The necessary adjustments are made exclusively in the methods `DimDown()`, `DimUp()`, `Off()` and `On()` of `FB_LampSetDirectDALIAdapter`.

The `On()` method is shown here as an example:

```
METHOD PUBLIC On
fbLampSetDirectDALI.SetLightLevel(254);
IF (_ipObserver <> 0) THEN
  _ipObserver.Update(TO_USINT(fbLampSetDirectDALI.nLightLevel
                              * 100.0 / 254.0));
END_IF
```

The adapter function block contains all the necessary instructions, which causes the DALI lamp to behave to the outside as expected. `FB_LampSetDirectDALI` remains unchanged with this solution approach.

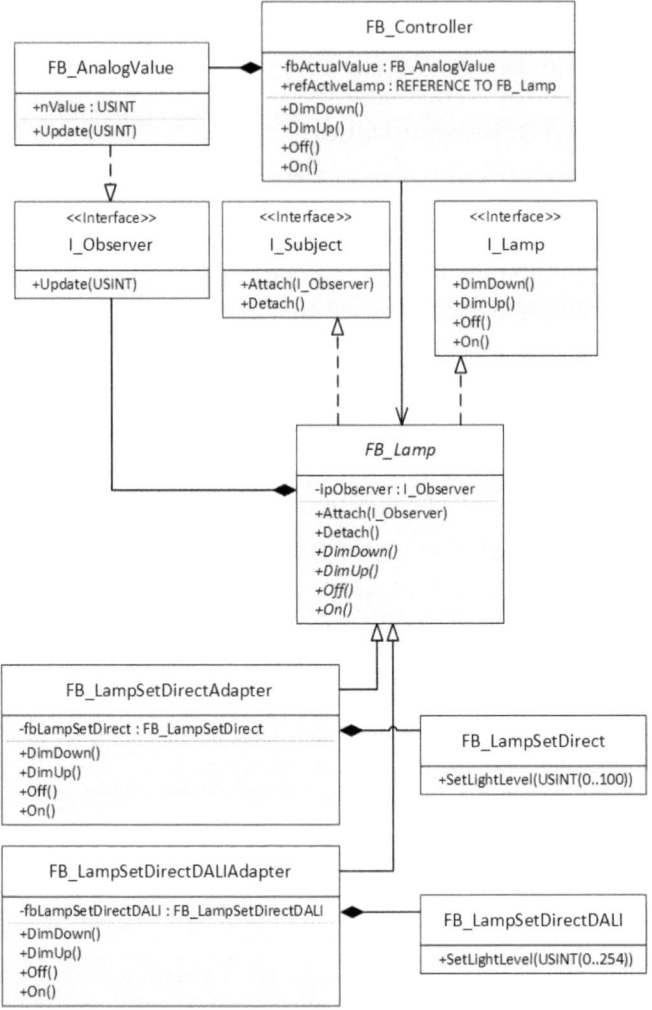

The example is available for download for TwinCAT 3.1 on GitHub[13].

---

[13] https://github.com/StefanHenneken/Blog-2022-04-IEC61131-LSP-Sample03

6.4 Optimization analysis

Through various techniques, it is possible for us to implement the desired extension without violating the *Liskov Substitution Principle*. Inheritance is a precondition to violate the *Liskov Substitution Principle*. If the *Liskov Substitution Principle* is violated, this may be an indication of a bad inheritance hierarchy within the software design.

Why is it important to follow the *Liskov Substitution Principle*? Function blocks can also be passed as parameters. If a POU would expect a parameter of the type `FB_LampSetDirect`, then `FB_LampSetDirectDALI` could also be passed when using inheritance. However, the operation of the `SetLightLevel()` method is different for the two function blocks. Such differences can lead to undesirable behavior within a system.

6.5 The definition of the Liskov Substitution Principle

> *Let q(x) be a property provable about objects x of type T. Then q(y) should be true for objects y of type S where S is a subtype of T.*

This is the more formal definition of the *Liskov Substitution Principle* by Barbara Liskov. As mentioned above, this principle was already defined at the end of the 1980s. The complete elaboration was published under the title *Data Abstraction and Hierarchy* [14].

Barbara Liskov was one of the first women to earn a doctorate in computer science in 1968. In 2008, she was also one of the first women to receive the Turing Award. Early on, she became involved with object-oriented programming and thus also with the inheritance of classes (function blocks).

---

[14] https://www.cs.tufts.edu/~nr/cs257/archive/barbara-liskov/data-abstraction-and-hierarchy.pdf

Inheritance places two function blocks in a specific relationship to each other. Inheritance here describes an is-a relationship. If `FB_LampSetDirectDALI` inherits from `FB_LampSetDirect`, the DALI lamp is a (normal) lamp extended by special (additional) functions. Wherever `FB_LampSetDirect` is used, `FB_LampSetDirectDALI` could also be used. `FB_LampSetDirect` can be substituted by `FB_LampSetDirectDALI`. If this is not ensured, the inheritance should be questioned at this point.

Robert C. Martin has included this principle in the SOLID principles. In the book *Clean Architecture: A Craftsman's Guide to Software Structure and Design*, this principle is explained further and extended to the field of software architecture.

6.6 Summary

By extending the above example, you have learned about the *Liskov Substitution Principle*. Complex inheritance hierarchies in particular are prone to violating this principle. Although the formal definition of the *Liskov Substitution Principle* sounds complicated, the key message of this principle is simple to understand.

7   The Interface Segregation Principle

The basic idea of the *Interface Segregation Principle* has strong similarities with the *Single Responsibility Principle*: Modules with too many responsibilities can negatively influence the maintenance and maintainability of a software system. The *Interface Segregation Principle* focuses on the module's interface. A module should implement only those interfaces that are needed for its task. The following shows how this design principle can be implemented.

7.1   Starting situation

In the last chapter about the *Liskov Substitution Principle*, the example was extended by another lamp type (`FB_LampSetDirectDALI`). The special feature of this lamp type is the scaling of the output value. While the other lamp types output 0-100%, the new lamp type outputs a value from 0 to 254.

Just like all other lamp types, the new lamp type (DALI lamp) has an adapter (`FB_LampSetDirectDALIAdapter`). The adapters have been added during the implementation of the *Single Responsibility Principle* and ensure that the function blocks of the individual lamp types are only responsible for a single function.

The sample program was last adapted so that the output value from the new lamp type (`FB_LampSetDirectDALI`) is scaled within the adapter from 0-254 to 0-100 %. This makes the DALI lamp behave exactly like the other lamp types without violating the *Liskov Substitution Principle*.

This will serve as a starting point for explaining the *Interface Segregation Principle*.

7.2   Extension of the implementation

Also this time, the application has to be extended. However, it is not a new lamp type that is defined, but an existing lamp type is extended by a functionality. The DALI lamp should be able to count the operating hours. For this purpose, the function block `FB_LampSetDirectDALI` is extended by the property `nOperatingTime`:

```
PROPERTY PUBLIC nOperatingTime : DINT
```

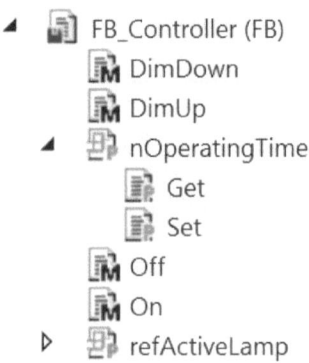

The setter can be used to set the operating hours counter to any value, while the getter returns the current state of the operating hours counter.

Since `FB_Controller` represents the individual lamp types, this function block is also extended by `nOperatingTime`:

The operating hours are recorded in the `FB_LampSetDirectDALI` function block. If the output value is > 0, the operating hours counter is incremented by 1 every second:

```
IF (nLightLevel > 0) THEN
  tonDelay(IN := TRUE, PT := T#1S);
  IF (tonDelay.Q) THEN
    tonDelay(IN := FALSE);
    _nOperatingTime := _nOperatingTime + 1;
  END_IF
ELSE
```

```
   tonDelay(IN := FALSE);
END_IF
```

The variable `_nOperatingTime` is the backing variable for the new property `nOperatingTime` and is declared in the function block.

What possibilities are there to transfer the value of `nOperatingTime` from `FB_LampSetDirectDALI` to the property `nOperatingTime` of `FB_Controller`? Here, too, there are now various approaches of integrating the required extension into the given software structure.

7.2.1 Approach 1: Extension of I_Lamp

The property for the new feature is integrated into the `I_Lamp` interface. Thus, the abstract function block `FB_Lamp` also receives the `nOperatingTime` property. Since all adapters inherit from `FB_Lamp`, the adapters of all lamp types receive this property, regardless of whether the lamp type supports an operating hours counter or not.

The getter and the setter of `nOperatingTime` in `FB_Controller` can thus directly access `nOperatingTime` of the individual adapters of the lamp types. The getter of `FB_Lamp` (abstract function block from which all adapters inherit) returns the value -1. The absence of the operating hours counter can thus be detected:

```
IF (fbController.nOperatingTime >= 0) THEN
  nOperatingTime := fbController.nOperatingTime;
ELSE
  // service not supported
END_IF
```

Since `FB_LampSetDirectDALI` supports the operating hours counter, the adapter (`FB_LampSetDirectDALIAdapter`) overwrites the `nOperatingTime` property. The getter and the setter from the adapter access `nOperatingTime` from `FB_LampSetDirectDALI`. In this way, the value of the operating hours counter is passed on to `FB_Controller`.

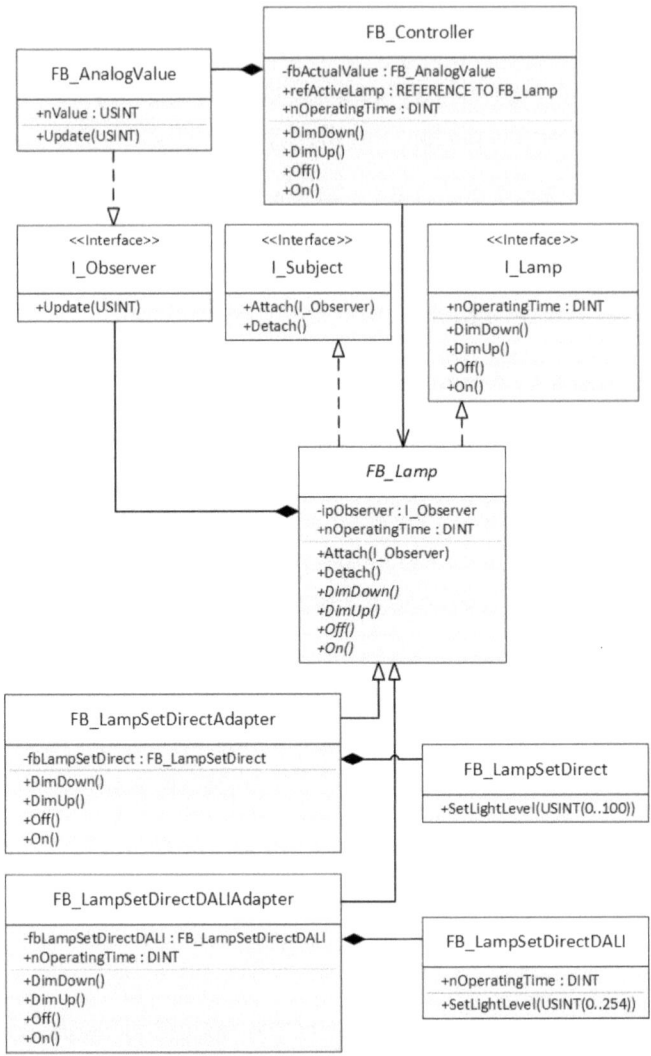

The example is available for download for TwinCAT 3.1 on GitHub[15].

This approach implements the feature as desired. Also, none of the SOLID principles shown so far are violated.

---

[15] https://github.com/StefanHenneken/Blog-2022-06-IEC61131-ISP-Sample01

However, the central interface `I_Lamp` is extended only to add another feature for one lamp type. All other adapters of the lamp types, even those that do not support the new feature, also receive the `nOperatingTime` property via the abstract base `FB_Lamp`.

With each feature that is added in this way, the interface `I_Lamp` increases and so does the abstract base `FB_Lamp`.

7.2.2 Approach 2: Additional Interface

In this approach, the `I_Lamp` interface is not extended, but a new interface (`I_OperatingTime`) is added for the desired functionality. `I_OperatingTime` contains only the property necessary for providing the operating hours counter:

```
PROPERTY PUBLIC nOperatingTime : DINT
```

This interface is implemented by the adapter `FB_LampSetDirectDALIAdapter`:

```
FUNCTION_BLOCK PUBLIC FB_LampSetDirectDALIAdapter
                       EXTENDS FB_Lamp
                       IMPLEMENTS I_OperatingTime
```

Thus, `FB_LampSetDirectDALIAdapter` receives the property `nOperationTime` not via `FB_Lamp` or `I_Lamp`, but via the new interface `I_OperatingTime`.

If `FB_Controller` accesses the active lamp type in the getter of `nOperationTime`, it is checked before the access whether the selected lamp type implements the `I_OperatingTime` interface. If this is the case, the property is accessed via `I_OperatingTime`. If the lamp type does not implement the interface, -1 is returned:

```
VAR
   ipOperatingTime : I_OperatingTime;
END_VAR
IF (__ISVALIDREF(_refActiveLamp)) THEN
   IF (__QUERYINTERFACE(_refActiveLamp, ipOperatingTime)) THEN
      nOperatingTime := ipOperatingTime.nOperatingTime;
   ELSE
      nOperatingTime := -1; // service not supported
   END_IF
END_IF
```

The setter of `nOperationTime` is structured similarly. After the successful check whether `I_OperatingTime` is implemented by the active lamp, the property is accessed via the interface:

```
VAR
   ipOperatingTime : I_OperatingTime;
END_VAR
IF (__ISVALIDREF(_refActiveLamp)) THEN
   IF (__QUERYINTERFACE(_refActiveLamp, ipOperatingTime)) THEN
      ipOperatingTime.nOperatingTime := nOperatingTime;
   END_IF
END_IF
```

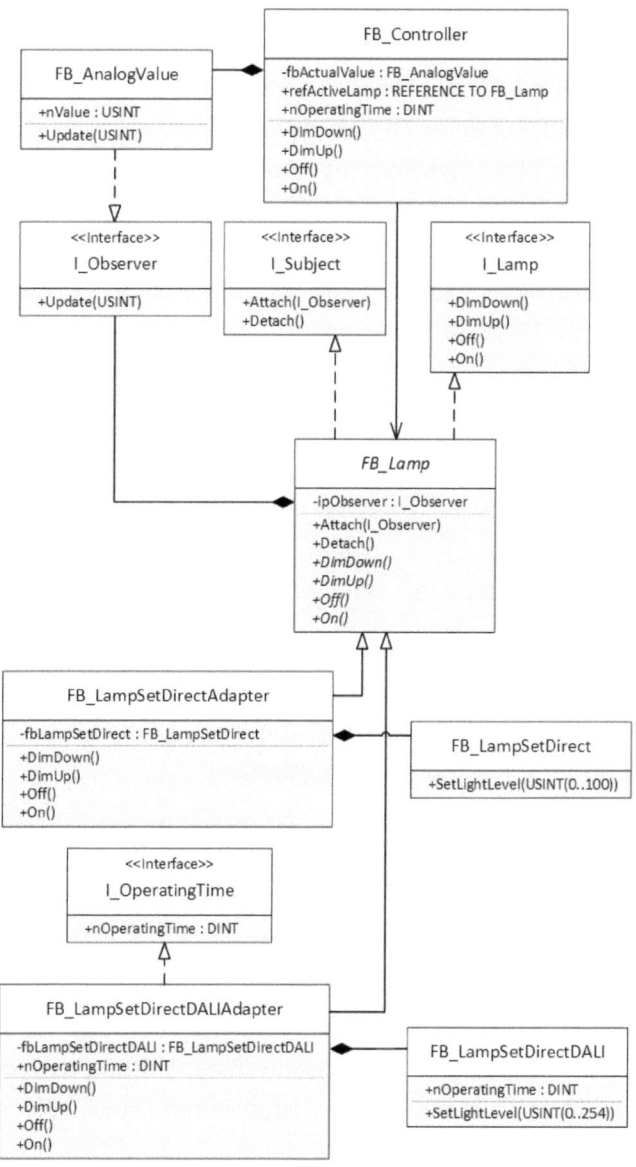

The example is available for download for TwinCAT 3.1 on GitHub[16].

---

[16] https://github.com/StefanHenneken/Blog-2022-06-IEC61131-ISP-Sample02

7.3 Optimization analysis

The use of a separate interface for the additional feature corresponds to the „optionality" from the chapter The *Liskov Substitution Principle*. In the above example, it can be checked at runtime of the program (with `__QUERYINTERFACE()`) whether a specific interface is implemented and thus the respective feature is supported. Further features, like `bIsDALIDevice` from the „Optionality" example, are not necessary with this solution approach.

If a separate interface is offered for each feature or functionality, other lamp types can also implement this in order to implement the desired feature. If `FB_LampSetDirect` also has to receive an operating hours counter, `FB_LampSetDirect` must be extended by the property `nOperatingTime`. In addition, `FB_LampSetDirectAdapter` must implement the `I_OperatingTime` interface. All other function blocks, including `FB_Controller`, remain unchanged.

If the functionality of the operating hours counter changes and `I_OperatingTime` receives additional methods, only the function blocks that also support the feature must be adapted.

Examples of the *Interface Segregation Principle* can also be found in .NET. For example, .NET has the interface `IList`. This interface contains methods and properties for creating, modifying and reading listings. However, depending on the use case, it may be sufficient for the user to only read a listing. However, passing a listing through `IList` in this case would also provide methods to modify the listing. One can use the `IReadOnlyList` interface for these use cases. With this interface, a listing can only be read. Accidental modification of the data is therefore not possible.

Dividing functionalities into individual interfaces thus increases not only the maintainability but also the security of a software system.

7.4 The definition of the Interface Segregation Principle

This brings us to the definition of the *Interface Segregation Principle*:

> *A module that uses an interface should be presented with only those methods that the interface really needs.*

Or to put it another way:

> *Clients should not be forced to depend on methods they do not need.*

A software design can still be adapted at any time during its development cycles. So, if you feel that an interface contains too many functionalities, check whether segregation is possible.

A common argument against the *Interface Segregation Principle* is the increased number of interfaces. Of course, overengineering should always be avoided. A certain amount of experience can be helpful here.

Abstract function blocks also represent an interface (see `FB_Lamp`). An abstract function block can contain basic functions to which the user only adds the necessary details. It is not necessary to implement all the methods or properties yourself. Here also it is important not to burden the user with technicalities which are not necessary for his tasks. The set of abstract methods and properties should be as small as possible.

Adherence to the *Interface Segregation Principle* keeps interfaces between functional blocks as small as possible, reducing coupling between each functional block.

7.5 Summary

If a software system has to cover further performance features, reflect the new requirements and do not hastily extend existing interfaces. Check whether separate interfaces are not a better decision. The reward is a software system that is easier to maintain, to test and to extend.

8   The Open/Closed Principle

Inheritance is a popular method for reusing existing function blocks. It enables new methods and properties to be added or existing methods overwritten without requiring access to the source code for the base function block. Designing software so that it can be extended without modifying the existing code is the key concept behind the *Open/Closed Principle*. But using inheritance also has disadvantages. These disadvantages can be minimised by employing interfaces – and this is not the only advantage of this method.

To put it another way, software behaviour should be open to extension without needing to modify the software. Based on our example from my previous posts, we're going to develop a function block for managing lamp control sequences. We will then add additional functionality to extend this function block. We will use this example to illustrate the key concept underlying the *Open/Closed Principle*.

8.1   Starting situation

Our main starting point is the function block `FB_SequenceManager`. This provides access to the individual steps in a sequence via the `aSequence` property. The `Sort()` method provides a means to sort the list in accordance with various criteria.

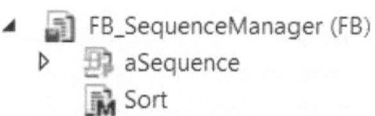

The `aSequence` property is an array and contains elements of type `ST_SequenceItem`:

```
PROPERTY PUBLIC aSequence : ARRAY [1..5] OF ST_SequenceItem
```

To keep our example simple, we define our array as having fixed upper and lower bounds of 1 and 5. Array elements are of type `ST_SequenceItem`, which contains a unique ID (`nId`), the output value for the lamps (`nValue`) and the duration (`nDuration`) before switching to the next output value:

```
TYPE ST_SequenceItem :
STRUCT
   nId         : UINT;
   nValue      : USINT(0..100);
   nDuration   : UINT;
END_STRUCT
END_TYPE
```

In this example, we will not concern ourselves with methods for processing the sequence. Our example does, however, include a `Sort()` method for sorting the list by various criteria:

```
METHOD PUBLIC Sort
VAR_INPUT
   eSortedOrder : E_SortedOrder;
END_VAR
```

The list can be sorted in ascending order only by nId or `nValue`:

```
TYPE E_SortedOrder :
(
   Id,
   Value
);
END_TYPE
```

In the `Sort()` method, the `eSortedOrder` input parameter determines whether the list is sorted by `nId` or `nValue`:

```
CASE eSortedOrder OF
   E_SortedOrder.Id:
      // Sort the list by nId
      // ...
   E_SortedOrder.Value:
      // Sort the list by nValue
      // ...
END_CASE
```

Our example is a simple monolithic application which can be put together quickly to meet our requirements.

The UML diagram shows the monolithic structure of the application very clearly:

FB_SequenceManager
+aSequence : ARRAY [1..5] OF ST_SequenceItem
+Sort(E_SortedOrder)

This does not, however, take account of the amount of work required to realise future extensions.

The example is available for download for TwinCAT 3.1 on GitHub[17].

8.2 Extension of the implementation

We are going to extend the application so that, in addition to `nId` and `nValue`, we can also sort the list by `nDuration`. Currently, the list is always sorted in ascending order. We would also like to be able to sort it in descending order.

How can we modify our example to meet these two client requirements?

8.2.1 Approach 1: Quick & Dirty

One approach is to simply extend the existing `Sort()` method so it can also sort by `nDuration`. To do this, we add the field `eDuration` to `E_SortedOrder`:

```
TYPE E_SortedOrder :
(
   Id,
   Value,
   Duration
);
END_TYPE
```

We also need a parameter to indicate whether we want to sort in ascending or descending order:

```
TYPE E_SortedDirection :
(
   Ascending,
   Descending
```

---

[17] https://github.com/StefanHenneken/Blog-2023-01-IEC61131-OCP-Sample01

```
);
END_TYPE
```

So the `Sort()` method now takes two parameters:

```
METHOD PUBLIC Sort
VAR_INPUT
  eSortedOrder       : E_SortedOrder;
  eSortedDirection   : E_SortedDirection;
END_VAR
```

The `Sort()` method now contains two nested CASE statements. The outermost of these deals with the sort direction, the innermost with the parameter by which to sort the list:

```
CASE eSortedDirection OF
  E_SortedDirection.Ascending:
    CASE eSortedOrder OF
      E_SortedOrder.Id:
        // Sort the list by nId in ascending order
        // ...
      E_SortedOrder.Value:
        // Sort the list by nValue in ascending order
        // ...
      E_SortedOrder.Duration:
        // Sort the list by nDuration in ascending order
        // ...
    END_CASE
  E_SortedDirection.Descending:
    CASE eSortedOrder OF
      E_SortedOrder.Id:
        // Sort the list by nId in descending order
        // ...
      E_SortedOrder.Value:
        // Sort the list by nValue in descending order
        // ...
      E_SortedOrder.Duration:
        // Sort the list by nDuration in descending order
        // ...
    END_CASE
  END_CASE
END_CASE
```

This approach is quick to implement. For a small application with a reasonably small amount of source code, this is absolutely a reasonable approach. But for this approach to be feasible, we have to have access to the source code. In addition, we need to ensure that `FB_SequenceManager` isn't shared with other projects via, for example, a PLC library containing `FB_SequenceManager`. By adding a parameter to the `Sort()` method, we have also changed its signature. This means that program components that call this method with just a single parameter will no longer compile.

The UML diagram shows clearly that the structure is unchanged – it's still a highly monolithic application:

FB_SequenceManager
+aSequence : ARRAY [1..5] OF ST_SequenceItem
+Sort(E_SortedOrder, E_SortedDirection)

The example is available for download for TwinCAT 3.1 on GitHub[18].

8.2.2   Approach 2: Inheritance

Another way to add features to the application is to use inheritance. This allows us to extend function blocks without having to modify the existing function block.

We start by creating a new function block which inherits from `FB_SequenceManager`:

```
FUNCTION_BLOCK PUBLIC FB_SequenceManagerEx
                          EXTENDS FB_SequenceManager
```

The new function block contains a `SortEx()` method which takes two parameters specifying the required sort direction and order:

```
METHOD PUBLIC SortEx : BOOL
VAR_INPUT
   eSortedOrder      : E_SortedOrderEx;
   eSortedDirection  : E_SortedDirection;
END_VAR
```

Once again we add a data type `E_SortedDirection` which specifies whether the list should be sorted in ascending or descending order:

---

[18] https://github.com/StefanHenneken/Blog-2023-01-IEC61131-OCP-Sample02

```
TYPE E_SortedDirection :
(
  Ascending,
  Descending
);
END_TYPE
```

Rather than extending `E_SortedOrder`, we create a new data type:

```
TYPE E_SortedOrderEx :
(
  Id,
  Value,
  Duration
);
END_TYPE
```

We can now implement the required sort functions in the `SortEx()` method.

To sort in ascending order, we can use the `Sort()` method from the base function block (`FB_SequenceManager`). We don't need to reimplement the existing sorting algorithm. All we need to do is add the additional sort type:

```
CASE eSortedOrder OF
  E_SortedOrderEx.Id:
    SUPER^.Sort(E_SortedOrder.Id);
  E_SortedOrderEx.Value:
    SUPER^.Sort(E_SortedOrder.Value);
  E_SortedOrderEx.Duration:
    // Sort the list by nDuration in ascending order
    // ...
END_CASE
```

Sorting in descending order needs to be programmed from scratch, however, as this cannot be achieved using existing methods.

If a new function block extends an existing function block, the new function block inherits the functionality of the base function block. The addition of further methods and properties enables it to be extended without needing to modify the base function block (open for extension). By using libraries, it's also possible to protect the source code from modification (closed for modification).

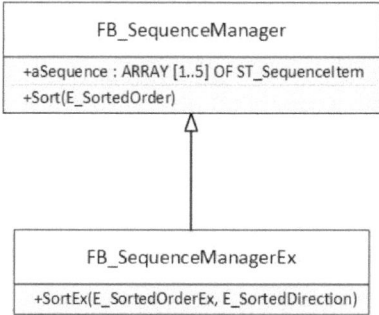

Inheritance is therefore one way of implementing the *Open/Closed Principle*.

The example is available for download for TwinCAT 3.1 on GitHub[19].

This approach does, however, have two disadvantages:

Excessive use of inheritance can end up generating complex hierarchies. A child function block is absolutely dependent on its base function block. If new methods or properties are added to the base function block, every child function block will also inherit these new elements (if they are PUBLIC), even if the child function block has no intention of exposing these elements externally.

In some circumstances, extension by inheritance is only possible where the child function block has access to internal state information from the base function block. Access to these internal elements can be enabled by marking them as PROTECTED. This restricts access to child function blocks only.

In the example given above, the only reason we were able to add the sorting algorithms was because the setter for the aSequence property was declared as PROTECTED. If we did not have write access to the aSequence property, the child function block would not be able to modify the list, so would not be able to sort it.

---

[19] https://github.com/StefanHenneken/Blog-2023-01-IEC61131-OCP-Sample03

This means, however, that the developer coding this function block always has to take into consideration two use cases. Firstly, a user making use of the function block's public methods and properties. Secondly, users using the function block as a base function block and adding new functionality via PROTECTED elements. But which internal elements need to be marked as PROTECTED? And to enable their use, these elements also need to be documented.

8.2.3 Approach 3: Additional interface

Another approach is to use interfaces rather than inheritance. This, however, needs to be considered during the design phase.

If FB_SequenceManager is to be designed so that the user of the function block can add any sorting algorithms, the code for sorting the list should be removed from FB_SequenceManager. The sorting algorithm should instead access the list via an interface.

In our example, we would add the interface I_SequenceSortable. This interface contains the SortList() method, which contains a reference to the list to be sorted:

```
METHOD SortList
VAR_INPUT
  refSequence : REFERENCE TO ARRAY [1..5] OF ST_SequenceItem;
END_VAR
```

Next we create the function blocks containing the various sorting algorithms, each of which implements the I_SequenceSortable interface. As an example, we will take the function block for sorting by nId in ascending order:

```
FUNCTION_BLOCK PUBLIC FB_SequenceSortedByIdAscending
                          IMPLEMENTS I_SequenceSortable
```

We can call the function block whatever we want; the crucial point is that it implements the I_SequenceSortable interface. This ensures that

FB_SequenceSortedByIdAscending contains the SortList() method. The actual sorting algorithm is implemented in the SortList() method:

```
METHOD SortList
VAR_INPUT
  refSequence : REFERENCE TO ARRAY [1..5] OF ST_SequenceItem;
END_VAR
// Sort the list by nId in ascending order
// ...
```

The Sort() method of FB_SequenceManager takes a parameter of type I_SequenceSortable. When calling the Sort() method we pass to it a function block (e.g. FB_SequenceSortedByIdAscending) which implements the I_SequenceSortable interface and therefore also contains the SortList() method. FB_SequenceManager's Sort() method calls SortList() and passes to it a reference to the aSequence list:

```
METHOD PUBLIC Sort
VAR_INPUT
  ipSequenceSortable     : I_SequenceSortable;
END_VAR
IF (ipSequenceSortable <> 0) THEN
  ipSequenceSortable.SortList(THIS^._aSequence);
END_IF
```

This means that a reference to the list to be sorted is passed to the function block containing the implemented sorting algorithm.

We create a separate function block for each sorting algorithm. This means we have access both to FB_SequenceManager containing the Sort() method, and to function blocks containing the sorting algorithms and implementing the I_SequenceSortable interface.

▲ 🗔 FB_SequenceManager (FB)
  ▷ 🗐 aSequence
    🗐 Sort
▲ 🗔 FB_SequenceSortedByDurationAscending (FB)
    🗐 SortList
▲ 🗔 FB_SequenceSortedByDurationDescending (FB)
    🗐 SortList
▲ 🗔 FB_SequenceSortedByIdAscending (FB)
    🗐 SortList
▲ 🗔 FB_SequenceSortedByIdDescending (FB)
    🗐 SortList
▲ 🗔 FB_SequenceSortedByValueAscending (FB)
    🗐 SortList
▲ 🗔 FB_SequenceSortedByValueDescending (FB)
    🗐 SortList
▲ 🗔° I_SequenceSortable
    🗐 SortList

When it calls the `Sort()` method, `FB_SequenceManager` passes to it a function block (in our case `FB_SequenceSortedByIdAscending`). This function block contains the `I_SequenceSortable` interface subsequently used to call the `SortList()` method:

```
PROGRAM MAIN
VAR
   fbSequenceManager                 : FB_SequenceManager;
   fbSequenceSortedByIdAscending :
                            FB_SequenceSortedByIdAscending;
   // ...
END_VAR
fbSequenceManager.Sort(fbSequenceSortedByIdAscending);
// ...
```

This approach avoids the use of inheritance. The sorting algorithm function blocks could employ their own inheritance hierarchy if required. These function blocks could also implement additional interfaces, since it is possible to implement multiple interfaces.

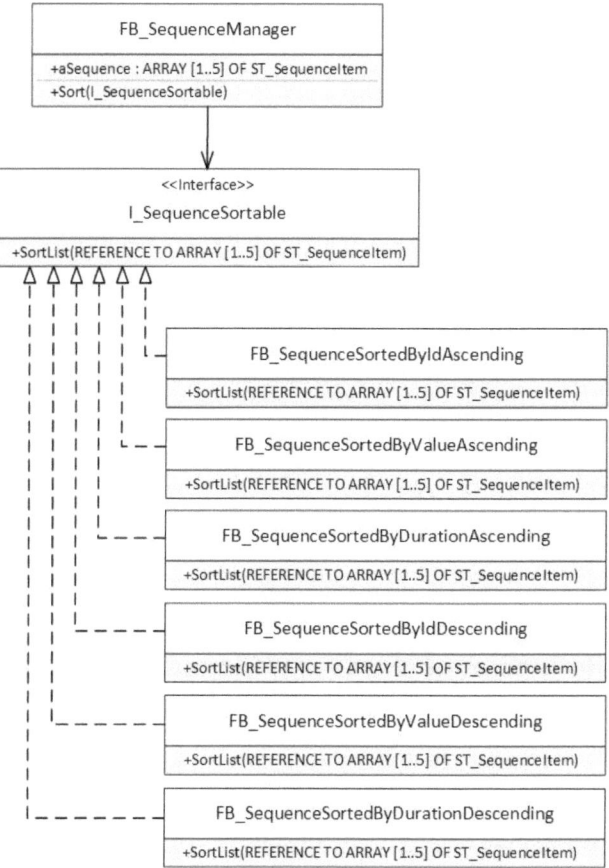

Using this interface realises a clear separation between data storage (the list) and data processing (sorting). The aSequence property does not need write access. We also avoid the need to access internal FB_SequenceManager variables.

In addition, we no longer need the E_SortedOrder and E_SortedDirection data types. The sort type is determined solely by which function block we pass to Sort().

We can also add new sorting algorithms without needing to modify or change existing elements.

The example is available for download for TwinCAT 3.1 on GitHub[20].

8.3 Optimization analysis

There are various methods for extending the functionally of an existing function block without having to modify it. As well as inheritance – a key feature of object-oriented programming (OOP) – interfaces may provide a better alternative.

Using interfaces brings greater decoupling. But the individual interfaces do have to be implemented in the software design. This means that we need to consider in advance which areas need to be abstracted via interfaces and which don't.

With inheritance too, when we develop a function block we have to consider which internal elements should be made accessible (by using the PROTECTED keyword) to function blocks derived from it.

8.4 The definition of the Open/Closed Principle

The *Open/Closed Principle* was originated in 1988 by Bertrand Meyer. It states:

> *Software entities should be open for extension,*
> *but closed for modification.*

Software entity: This means a class, function block, module, method, service, etc.

Open: The behaviour of a software entity should be able to be extended.

Closed: Extensibility shall not be achieved by modifying existing software.

When Bertrand Meyer defined the *Open/Closed Principle* in the late 1980s, the focus was on C++ as a programming language. He used the concept of

---

[20] https://github.com/StefanHenneken/Blog-2023-01-IEC61131-OCP-Sample04

inheritance, a familiar concept in the object-oriented programming world. Object-orientated programming – at the time a fairly young discipline – was seen as promising big improvements in terms of reusability and maintainability as a result of the ability to reuse classes as base classes for new classes.

When Robert C. Martin took up Meyer's principle in the 1990s, he took a different approach to its technical implementation. C++ allows the use of multiple inheritance, which is rare in more recent programming languages. Consequently, Robert C. Martin focused on the use of interfaces. More information can be found in his book *Clean Architecture: A Craftsman's Guide to Software Structure and Design*.

8.5 Summary

Adhering to the *Open/Closed Principle* does carry a risk of overengineering. We should only implement extensibility where it is actually needed. It is impossible to design software so that every conceivable extension can be implemented without needing to modify the source code.

9 Additional Principles

This concludes my series of posts on SOLID principles. In addition to the SOLID principles, however, there are other principles that are also briefly presented here. What all these principles have in common is the goal of making software more maintainable and more reusable.

9.1 Don't Repeat Yourself (DRY)

The DRY principle states (as the name suggests) that program code should not be duplicated unnecessarily. Instead, a function should be implemented only once and called at desired points in the program.

The DRY principle can help improve the maintainability of code, as it becomes easier to make changes to a function if it is implemented in only one place in the program code. In addition, the DRY principle can help reduce errors in the program, since duplicated code often leads to unexpected behaviour when a change is made in only one of the duplicated locations. Thus the DRY principle is an important principle in the software development, which can contribute to the improvement of the code quality.

Although the DRY principle is easy to understand and implement, it is probably the most disregarded principle. Because nothing is easier than to repeat source code by copy & paste. Especially when the time pressure is particularly high. Therefore, you should always try to implement shared functions in separate modules.

The following short example shows the application of the DRY principle. A PLC program receives different temperature values from several sensors. All temperature values are to be displayed in an HMI and written to a log file. To make the temperature values more readable, the formatting should be done in the PLC:

```
FUNCTION F_DisplayTemperature : STRING
VAR_INPUT
  fSensorValue    : LREAL;
  bFahrenheit     : BOOL;
```

```
END_VAR
IF (fSensorValue > 0) THEN
   IF (bFahrenheit) THEN
      F_DisplayTemperature := CONCAT('Temperature: ',
            REAL_TO_FMTSTR(fSensorValue, 1, TRUE));
      F_DisplayTemperature := CONCAT(F_DisplayTemperature,
                     ' °C');
   ELSE
      F_DisplayTemperature := CONCAT('Temperature: ',
            REAL_TO_FMTSTR(fSensorValue * 1.8 + 32, 1, TRUE));
      F_DisplayTemperature := CONCAT(F_DisplayTemperature,
                     ' °F');
   END_IF
ELSE
      F_DisplayTemperature := 'No sensor data available';
END_IF
```

In this example the function F_DisplayTemperature() is implemented only once. For the formatting of the temperature values this function is called at the desired places in the program. By avoiding duplicated code, the program becomes clearer and easier to read. If, for example, it is necessary to change the number of decimal places, this only has to be done in one place, namely in the function F_DisplayTemperature().

In addition to the use of functions, inheritance can also help to comply with the DRY principle by relocating a functionality in a base FB and using it by all derived FBs.

However, there may be cases in which the DRY principle should be deliberately violated. This is always the case if the readability of the source code is worsened by the use of DRY. Thus for the circle computation the formula for the circumference ($U = 2r\pi$) or for the area ($A = r^2\pi$) is sufficiently readable. An outsourcing into separate functions does not increase the code quality, but only the dependence to further modules, in which the functions for the circle computation are. Instead, a global constant should be created for π and used in the calculations.

In summary, the DRY principle helps make program code cleaner and shorter by avoiding code duplication.

9.2   Law Of Demeter (LoD)

The *Law of Demeter* is another principle whose observance can significantly minimize the couplings between function blocks. The *Law of Demeter* specifies that only elements in the immediate vicinity should be accessed from a function block (or method or function). In concrete terms, this means that only accesses to the following elements are permitted:

- Variables of the own function block (everything between `VAR/END_VAR`)

- Methods/properties of the own function block

- Methods/properties of the function blocks that were created in the own function block

- Parameters passed to methods or function blocks (`VAR_INPUT`)

- Global constants or parameters contained in a parameter list

The *Law of Demeter* could therefore also be called: Don't talk to strangers. **Strangers** are elements that are not directly present in the function block. In contrast, the own elements are called **friends**.

Also this principle originates from the 1980iger years, thus from the time, in which the object-oriented software development increased strongly in popularity. The name *Demeter* is to be led back on a software project of the same name, in which this principle was recognized for the first time (Demeter is in the Greek mythology the sister of Zeus and the Goddess of the agriculture). At the end of the 1980s, this principle was further elaborated by Ian Holland and Karl J. Lieberherr and published under the title *Assuring Good Style for Object-Oriented Programs* [21].

The following graphic is intended to illustrate the *Law of Demeter* in a little more detail:

---

[21] https://homepages.cwi.nl/~storm/teaching/reader/LieberherrHolland89.pdf

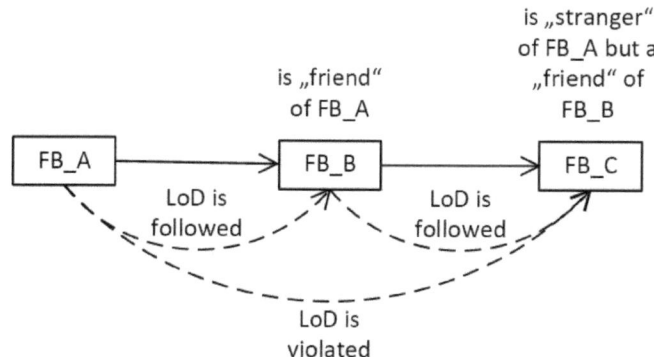

FB_A contains an instance of FB_B (fbB). Therefore, FB_A can directly access the methods and properties of FB_B.

FB_B contains an instance of FB_C. Therefore, FB_B can access FB_C directly.

FB_B could offer a property or a method that returns the reference to FB_C (refC). Access from FB_A to the instance of FB_C via FB_B would thus theoretically be possible:

```
nValue := fbB.refC.nValue;
```

The instance on FB_C is created in FB_B. If FB_A accesses this instance directly, a fixed coupling between FB_A and FB_C is created. This fixed coupling can lead to problems in the care, maintenance and testing of the program. If FB_A is tested, not only FB_B must be present, but FB_C as well. A frequent violation of the *Law of Demeter* is therefore also helpful in the early detection of maintenance problems.

Even creating a corresponding local variable in which the reference to FB_C is stored does not solve the actual problem:

```
refC    : REFERENCE TO FB_C;
refC REF= fbB.refC;
nValue := refC.nValue;
```

At first glance, these dependencies are not always apparent, as `FB_C` is accessed indirectly via `FB_B`.

Here is a concrete example that illustrates the problem again and also offers a solution.

The function blocks `FB_Building`, `FB_Floor`, `FB_Room` and `FB_Lamp` represent the structure of a building and its lighting. The building consists of 5 floors, each containing 20 rooms and each room contains 10 lamps.

Each function block contains the corresponding instances of the underlying elements. The function blocks each provide a property that offers a reference to these elements. `FB_Lamp` contains the property `nPowerConsumption`, via which the current power consumption of the lamp is output.

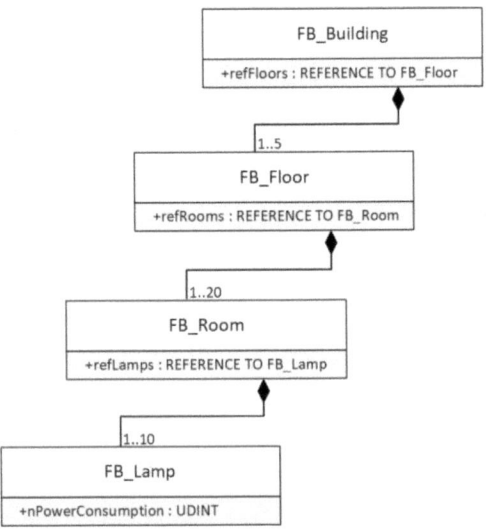

A function is to be developed that determines the power consumption of all lamps in the building.

One solution could be to access each individual lamp via several nested loops and add up the power consumption:

```
FUNCTION F_CalcPowerConsumption : UDINT
VAR_INPUT
  refBuilding              : REFERENCE TO FB_Building;
END_VAR
VAR
  nFloor, nRoom, nLamp   : INT;
END_VAR

IF (NOT __ISVALIDREF(refBuilding)) THEN
  F_CalcPowerConsumption := 0;
  RETURN;
END_IF
FOR nFloor := 1 TO 5 DO
  FOR nRoom := 1 TO 20 DO
    FOR nLamp := 1 TO 10 DO
      F_CalcPowerConsumption :=
               F_CalcPowerConsumption + refBuilding
                      .refFloors[nFloor]
                      .refRooms[nRoom]
                      .refLamps[nLamp].nPowerConsumption;
    END_FOR
  END_FOR
END_FOR
```

The „diving" into the object structure down to each lamp seems somehow impressive. But this makes the function dependent on all function blocks, even those that are only indirectly addressed via a reference.

The access of refBuilding to refFloors does not violate the *Law of Demeter*, since refFloors is a direct property of FB_Building. However, all further accesses to the references have the consequence that our function also becomes dependent on the other function blocks.

If, for example, the structure of FB_Room or FB_Floor changes, the function for power consumption may also have to be adapted.

To comply with the *Law of Demeter*, each function block could offer a method (CalcPowerConsumption()) in which the power consumption is calculated. In each of these methods, the underlying method CalcPowerConsumption() is called:

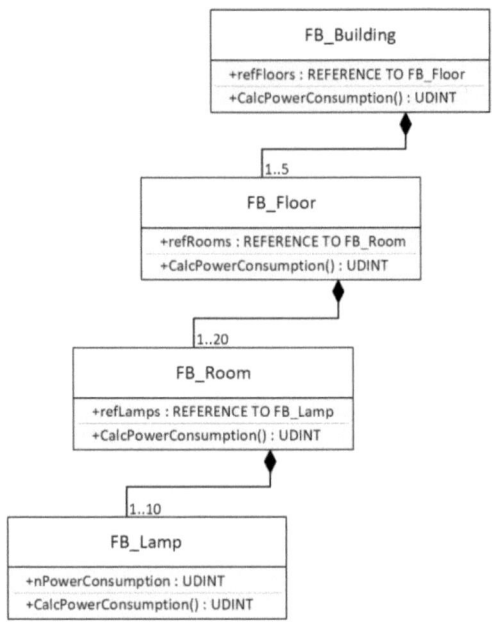

The `CalcPowerConsumption()` method in `FB_Building` only accesses its own elements. In this case, it accesses the property `refFloors` to call the method `CalcPowerConsumption()` of `FB_Floor`:

```
METHOD CalcPowerConsumption : UDINT
VAR
    nFloor    : INT;
END_VAR
FOR nFloor := 1 TO 5 DO
    CalcPowerConsumption := CalcPowerConsumption +
                    refFloors[nFloor].CalcPowerConsumption();
END_FOR
```

In `CalcPowerConsumption()` of `FB_Floor`, only `FB_Room` is accessed:

```
METHOD CalcPowerConsumption : UDINT
VAR
    nRoom    : INT;
END_VAR
FOR nRoom := 1 TO 20 DO
    CalcPowerConsumption := CalcPowerConsumption +
                    refRooms[nRoom].CalcPowerConsumption();
END_FOR
```

Finally, the power consumption of all lamps in the room is calculated in `FB_Room`:

```
METHOD CalcPowerConsumption : UDINT
VAR
  nLamp    : INT;
END_VAR
FOR nLamp := 1 TO 10 DO
  CalcPowerConsumption := CalcPowerConsumption +
                       refLamps[nLamp].nPowerConsumption;
END_FOR
```

The structure of the function `F_CalcPowerConsumption()` is thus much simpler:

```
FUNCTION F_CalcPowerConsumption : UDINT
VAR_INPUT
  refBuilding        : REFERENCE TO FB_Building;
END_VAR
IF (NOT __ISVALIDREF(refBuilding)) THEN
  F_CalcPowerConsumption := 0;
  RETURN;
END_IF
F_CalcPowerConsumption := refBuilding.CalcPowerConsumption();
```

After this adjustment, `F_CalcPowerConsumption()` is only dependent on `FB_Building` and its method `CalcPowerConsumption()`. How `FB_Building` calculates the power consumption in `CalcPowerConsumption()` is irrelevant for `F_CalcPowerConsumption()`. The structure of `FB_Room` or `FB_Floor` could change completely, `F_CalcPowerConsumption()` would not have to be adapted.

The first variant, in which all function blocks were iterated through, is very susceptible to changes. No matter which function block the structure changes, an adjustment of `F_CalcPowerConsumption()` would be necessary every time.

The example is available for download for TwinCAT 3.1 on GitHub[22].

---

[22] https://github.com/StefanHenneken/SOLID-Book-LoD-Sample01

However, it must be taken into account that nested structures do make sense. The *Law of Demeter* does not have to be applied here. It can be helpful to distribute the configuration data hierarchically over several structures in order to increase readability.

9.3   Keep It Simple, Stupid (KISS)

The KISS principle states that code should be as „simple" as possible so that it is as easy to understand as possible and thus effective to maintain. Here, „simple" is also to be understood as „plain". This means a simplicity that tries to leave out the unnecessary but still fulfils the customer's requirements. By following the KISS principle, a system is:

- easy to understand
- easy to extend
- easy to maintain

If the requirement is to sort ten million records, using the bubblesort algorithm would be simple to implement, but the low speed of the algorithm will not meet the client's requirements. Therefore, a solution must always be found that meets the customer's required expectations, but whose implementation is as simple (plain) as possible.

Basically, two types of requirements are to be distinguished:

Functional requirement: The customer or stakeholder demands a specific feature. The exact requirements for this feature are then defined together with the customer and only then is it implemented. Functional requirements extend an application with clear functions (features) desired by the customer.

Non-functional requirements: A non-functional requirement is, for example, the splitting of an application into different modules or the provision of interfaces, e.g. to enable unit tests. Non-functional requirements are performance features that are not necessarily visible to the customer. However, these may be necessary so that the software system can be maintained and serviced.

The KISS principle is always about the non-functional requirements. The focus is on the „how". In other words, the question of how the required functions are achieved. The YAGNI principle, which is described in the following chapter, refers to the **functional requirements**. Here the focus is on the „what".

The KISS principle can be applied at several levels:

Formatting source code

Although the following source code is very compact, the KISS principle is violated here because it is difficult to understand and thus very error-prone:

```
IF(x<=RT[k-1](o[n+2*j]))THEN WT[j+k](l AND NOT S.Q);END_IF;
IF(x>RI[k+1](o[n+2*k]))THEN WO[j-k](l OR NOT S.Q);END_IF;
```

The source code should be formatted in such a way that the sequence is better recognised. Also, the identifiers for variables and functions should be chosen in such a way that their meaning is easier to understand.

Unnecessary source code

Source code that does not help to improve readability also violates the KISS principle:

```
bCalc := F_CalcFoo();
IF (bCalc = TRUE) THEN
  bResult := TRUE;
ELSE
  bResult := FALSE;
END_IF
```

Although the source code is well structured and the identifiers have been chosen so that their meaning is easier to recognise, the source code can be significantly reduced:

```
bResult := F_CalcFoo();
```

This one line is much easier to understand than the 6 lines before. The source code is „simpler", with the same range of functions.

Software design / software architecture

The design or structure of software can also violate the KISS principle. If, for example, a complete SQL database is used to store configuration data, although a text file would suffice, the KISS principle is also violated.

The division of a PLC programme into several CPU cores only makes sense if it also produces a practical benefit. In this case, appropriate mechanisms must be built into a PLC program to synchronise access to shared resources. These increase the complexity of the system considerably and should only be used if the application requires them.

I have deliberately placed the two chapters on the KISS principle and the YAGNI principle at the end of the book. From here I would like to take a brief look back at the beginning of the book.

When introducing the SOLID principles, I occasionally pointed out the danger of overengineering. Abstractions should only be provided if they are necessary for the implementation of features.

To clarify this, I will use the example for the explanation of the SOLID principles again.

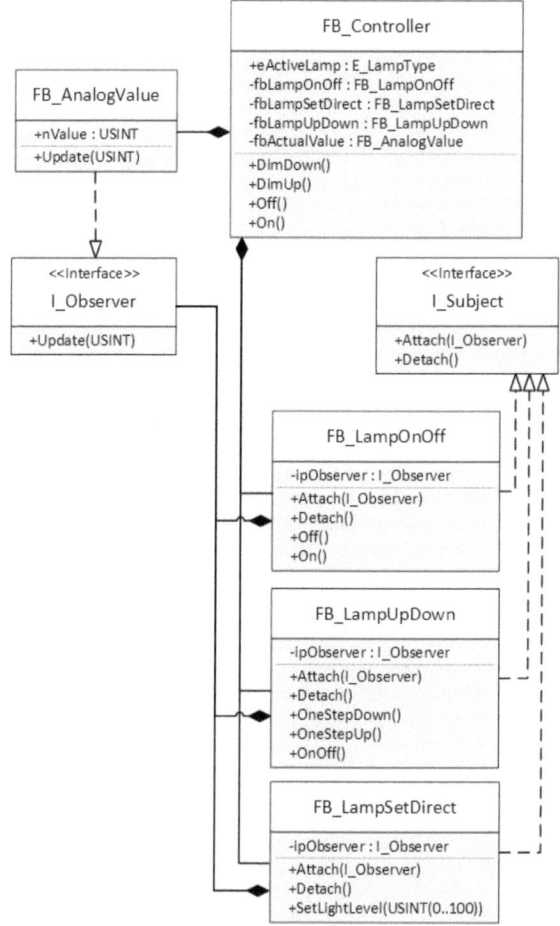

There is a fixed dependency between the three lamp types and the controller. If the application is to be extended by another lamp type, it is necessary to adapt the programme at various points. By applying the *Dependency Inversion Principle* and the *Single Responsibility Principle*, the programme became much more flexible. The integration of additional lamp types has been significantly simplified. However, the complexity of the programme was also significantly increased by these adjustments, as the UML diagram shows:

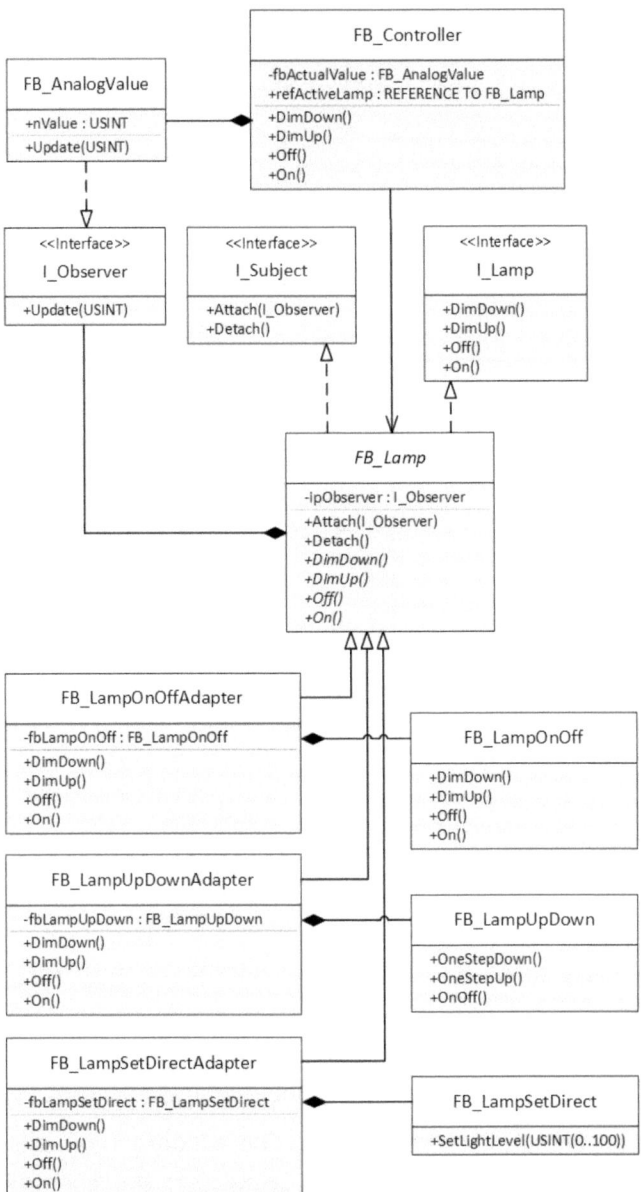

Before additional levels of abstraction are realised by applying the SOLID principles, one should always critically question the extra effort involved.

The structure of the first variant is completely sufficient if the program is used exclusively in a project to this extent. The program is small enough to understand the structure of the software and to make small adjustments. The KISS principle was followed. No more complexity than necessary has been built in.

However, if the first variant is only an intermediate step, e.g. in the development of a comprehensive light management system, it is to be expected that the application will increase in complexity. It is also possible that at a later stage the development will have to be distributed among several people. The use of unit tests is another point that justifies the implementation of SOLID principles. Without decoupling the individual lamp types through interfaces, the use of unit tests is difficult or even impossible. Here, too, the KISS principle is not violated. The KISS principle must therefore always be considered in context.

9.4   You Ain't Gonna Need It (YAGNI)

YAGNI stands for *You Ain't Gonna Need It* and also means *You will not need it*. It means that in software development you should only implement the features that are needed. No functions or features should be implemented, which might be needed someday.

In contrast to the KISS principle, which always focuses on the **non-functional requirements**, the YAGNI principle focuses on the **functional requirements**.

When developing software, it can be tempting to implement additional features without a concrete requirement. This can be the case, for example, if features are implemented during development without consulting the customer, in the firm belief that the customer will demand them later.

Referring to our example above, the YAGNI principle would be violated if the operating hours recording were implemented (see Chapter 7 - *The*

Interface Segregation Principle), although this was not requested by the customer.

If it is determined during development that a particular feature could be useful, it should only be implemented after consultation with the customer. Otherwise, a system will gradually receive more and more source code for features that no one needs.

This example makes it clear once again that all the principles described here in the book are not fixed rules or even laws. However, the principles are a powerful tool for improving the code quality of software.

10 Index